BLESSED

BROKEN

GIVEN

How Your Story Becomes Sacred
in the Hands of Jesus

GLENN PACKIAM

MULTNOMAH

Details in some anecdotes and stories have been changed to protect the identities of the persons involved.

Trade Paperback ISBN 978-0-525-65075-1
eBook ISBN 978-0-525-65089-8

Cover design by Mark D. Ford

Published in the United States by Multnomah, an imprint of the Crown Publishing Group, a division of Penguin Random House LLC, New York.

MULTNOMAH® and its mountain colophon are registered trademarks of Penguin Random House LLC.

Library of Congress Cataloging-in-Publication Data
Names: Packiam, Glenn, author.
Title: Blessed broken given : how your story becomes sacred in the hands of Jesus / Glenn Packiam
Description: First Edition. | Colorado Springs : Multnomah, 2019. | Includes bibliographical references.
Identifiers: LCCN 2018055369 | ISBN 9780525650751 (pbk.) | ISBN 9780525650898 (electronic)
Subjects: LCSH: Christian life. | Christian biography.
Classification: LCC BV4501.3 .P3228 2019 | DDC 248.4—dc23
LC record available at https://lccn.loc.gov/2018055369

Printed in the United States of America
2019—First Edition

10 9 8 7 6 5 4 3 2 1

SPECIAL SALES
Most Multnomah books are available at special quantity discounts when purchased in bulk by corporations, organizations, and special-interest groups. Custom imprinting or excerpting can also be done to fit special needs. For information, please email specialmarketscms@penguinrandomhouse.com or call 1-800-603-7051.

"This book immerses us in the miraculous story of God, who uses broken and frail humans regardless of their past failures, present realities, or future struggles—all for His glory and our joy. There is nothing common or ordinary about life in Jesus. As you read this book, I pray you'd be able to see the seemingly mundane and ordinary things in your life with new eyes. It is in the common, the small, and the ordinary in which the creator of the universe is joyfully at work."

—MATT CHANDLER, lead pastor of the Village Church

"Glenn Packiam is a rare gem—budding academic, songwriter, Anglican priest, charismatic pastor, and fantastic writer. To have Glenn's mind and heart aimed at the Table, the locus of the church, is a gift to the church at large. This book is well worth your time."

—JOHN MARK COMER, pastor for teaching and vision at Bridgetown Church and author of *The Ruthless Elimination of Hurry*

"In our world of technology and isolation, we long not just for truth about God but for His personal touch. Glenn has opened a window into our hearts and minds so that we might understand the beauty of life and the love of a Father who is so willing to pour out for us every day. A brilliant book!"

—SALLY CLARKSON, speaker and author of *The Lifegiving Home, Own Your Life,* and *Different*

"Meditate on this: 'In the hands of Jesus, your life becomes broken in a new way. When you place the brokenness of your failure, frailty, and suffering in Jesus's hands, you become open to the grace of God.' My friend Glenn wrote these beautiful, life-giving words. This book is a treasure chest overflowing with life-transforming wisdom."

—DR. DERWIN L. GRAY, lead pastor of Transformation Church and author of *Limitless Life*

"Packiam's triple emphasis—blessed, broken, given—is a combination of three beautiful terms, each explained with Scripture, dipped in theology, and illustrated with narrative. *Blessed Broken Given* is a book for study groups to read and pray over together to turn this meal into the glory God has given us."

—Rev. Canon Dr. Scot McKnight, professor
of New Testament at Northern Seminary

"This book was written out of years of learning and practice. My friend Glenn embodies everything on these pages and lives a life that demands our attention. You'll find yourself more in love with Jesus as you embrace the timeless truths of this book."

—Brady Boyd, senior pastor of New Life Church
and author of *Remarkable*

"*Blessed Broken Given* is a brilliant, beautiful, thoughtful introduction to sacramental thought and practice for those hungering for a deeper, more tangible encounter with God and His world. It blends academic rigor with the imagination of a musician and the generous heart of a practicing pastor. I highly recommend it."

—Pete Greig, cofounder of 24-7 Prayer International, senior
pastor of Emmaus Rd, and author of *Dirty Glory*

"Packiam develops the powerful image of our lives as bread. Reflective yet practical, this is a super exploration of an important theme."

—Andrew Wilson, teaching pastor at King's Church London

"Glenn Packiam is one of the most insightful and compelling voices in North America. He offers us a powerful yet ordinary vision of what Jesus wants to do with our lives, if we would be bread in His hands. A good way of starting this journey of living blessed, broken, and given is to get this book in your hands!"

—Rich Villodas, lead pastor of New Life Fellowship

"This book provides manna in the wilderness to countless Christians hungry for a deeper walk with God. Fresh and engaging, it offers a gracious invitation to place your life in the hands of Jesus so that you may be blessed, broken, and given for the life of the world."

—Dr. Winfield Bevins, director of church planting
at Asbury Theological Seminary and author
of *Ever Ancient, Ever New*

To my wife, Holly, who is gluten-free
and tries to avoid eating bread.

Contents

Prelude

Glorious Bread

Is there anything more ordinary than bread? It's a building block of a meal. The French have baguettes and croissants, Chinese have steamed rolls stuffed with delicious meats, Indians have naan and chapati, Mexicans have tortillas, English have scones, and Americans have sliced white bread.

I grew up in Malaysia, where roti was my daily bread. *Roti* is technically just the Malay word for *bread,* but the word is often used to refer to a specific kind of flatbread—a more buttery and flaky version of naan, which is like a thicker, fluffier version of a tortilla. Roti can be eaten for breakfast, lunch, or dinner, and there were days when I proved it.

In my teen years—when I was completing high school via a distance-learning program with an American Christian school—I would get up in the morning, walk around the corner to the nearby restaurant, and have roti and dal (basically a lentil curry) for breakfast. And if I was hungry again at lunchtime, I'd repeat the ritual. I suspect that next to rice, roti is the food that Malaysians eat more than any other.

For all its different names and various forms, bread is the global common meal.

It is the very commonness of bread that accounts for its appearance again and again in Scripture. It isn't bread's spectacular or unique features that contribute to its prominence. It is its ordinariness, its "mere-ness." It is *just* bread.

And that's what makes it the perfect metaphor for our lives. Because if we're honest, most of what we do is ordinary. The everyday sleeping, waking, teeth-brushing, cleaning-the-house activities are common to everyone. We all get up, go to work—paid or unpaid—tinker at our hobbies, and try to do our best. We all shuttle kids around, mow the lawn, and shop for groceries. We all try to make sure the accounts balance and the checks clear. Not much about our daily lives sets us apart from the people around us. It's just *life*. Like bread. Is there anything more ordinary?

Most of us respond to the ordinary and mundane repetitions of life in one of three ways.

Some of us resign ourselves to second-class existence—to being among the unlucky masses who lead merely ordinary lives, who participate in meaningful work only marginally, and who show up at church just to cheer on the holy and the called. We applaud influential and remarkable people, while quietly admitting that will never be *us*. There is nothing uncommon about our lives, so what's the point in trying?

Or we strive, press, and push—trying to will our best future to reality. We read books about making our lives count, discovering our purpose, and becoming the heroes of our own stories. There's an adventure we were made to live, and we're going to embrace it in order to leave our mark on the world. We want God to be our agent who believes in us, promotes us, and makes our dreams come true. We want the Holy Spirit to be our super-caffeinated drink that fuels our frenzied pace. Life is an uphill climb, but doggone it, we don't want to climb—we want to fly. That is, until we come crashing down in sheer exhaustion because it's all just too much.

The third approach is even more dire. Rather than settling or beating relentlessly against the wind, perhaps we see ourselves as stained and flawed, messed up and imperfect. We're not just ordi-nary; we're *less than that.* There have been too many failures, too many disappointments, too much pain. Others seem to shine and succeed; everything they touch turns to gold. But not us. Nothing seems to work quite right for us. We always seem to come up short. And there's a gnawing in our guts that we're trying to ig-nore, a voice that gets louder each day: *It's too late. I've missed my moment and missed the mark.* We can't help feeling as if our lives have passed their use-by dates, like stale bread.

How do you see yourself? Have you settled for a life that may not matter much? Or are you living with an unsustainable manic optimism? Are you striving and straining, grasping and grabbing for something that always feels *just* out of reach? Perhaps you're wrestling with an unkind and deeply troubling voice—the one that says that you just don't matter, that you're "less than" and "never enough."

I have good news for you. There is more to this life than what you see. There is more to *you* than what you see. *Nothing in this world is as common as it seems.*

Even bread is really more than bread.

In the Bible bread is not simply a dietary staple, a common food consumed daily. Bread is a picture of God's provision, the sustenance that arrives from His hand. In the wilderness it fell from the sky, providing day-to-day nourishment for the people of Israel. But even when they entered the Promised Land and began to cultivate the ground, planting and harvesting, raising crops and livestock, they were to see God and not their own effort as the source of their provision. As every mealtime Hebrew prayer reminded them, God was the giver of bread.

Bread also became a guiding metaphor for the Torah—the law of the Lord. Just as bread came from heaven to feed the Israelites in the desert, so the instructions of the Lord came to Moses on the mountain. The people were to feed on these commandments; they could not live on "bread alone" but on "every word that comes from the mouth of the LORD" (Deuteronomy 8:3). Daily manna was a metaphor for practical guidance as they walked continually as the covenant people of God. They were to consume the scroll of the Word of the Lord as one consumes bread.

Bread is also the way Jesus demonstrated compassion to the crowd hanging on His every word. He fed them, spiritually and physically. In fact, Jesus went so far as to call Himself the "Bread of Life," the Bread that came down from heaven. This imagery reaches its fullest expression when Jesus, on the night of His death, took bread, gave thanks to the Father, and said to His disciples, "Take, eat; this is my body" (Matthew 26:26).

Bread became the way the church commemorates and remembers, experiences and encounters Jesus—Christ, the crucified, risen, and returning one. The sacrament of the Lord's Table is one of wine and bread.

Bread, as it turns out, is far from merely ordinary.

And so it is with our lives.

God works with the unspectacular and common, the imperfect and inadequate. That is His specialty. If God were to take the seemingly ordinary stuff of your life and fill it with His glory, He would not be working against the order of the world; He would be making your life what it was designed to be—a carrier of His glory.

FILLED WITH GLORY

Malaysia is a swirl of cultural influences, from the Portuguese and Dutch hundreds of years earlier to the British only decades ago to traders from India and China. The Southeast Asian–Euro fusion shows up in food, languages, and architecture. We lived on a row of terrace houses, houses that all shared a brick wall to the left and the right and yet had iron gates at the entrance of each individual driveway. Our house had no backyard, just a patio of sorts with an outdoor kitchen to prepare fragrant Asian meals and a place to hang up laundry to dry. The patio looked down to an alleyway that few people chose to walk through.

We had a small front garden with a papaya tree, a little red palm tree, and a variety of vibrant tropical flowers. Across the street, beyond our iron gate, there was a half-uprooted tree stump that lay almost parallel to the ground. And there was a large stone nestled near it, which seemed to be a perfect seat. The first time I took my place on the stump by the stone, I knew it was no ordinary spot. I was sitting in a spaceship, the *Millennium Falcon* actually. Many afternoons in my boyhood were spent flying at warp speed through the galaxy, dodging enemy fighters and rescuing fellow pilots.

The imagination of a child is one of the most powerful forces in the galaxy.

But something happens as we grow up. Tree stumps and stones become just tree stumps and stones. The world is not as magical as it once was. Things become ordinary. And the older we get, the more ordinary life seems. Where we once dreamed of changing the world, we find ourselves occupied with changing diapers and flat tires. Where our conversations used to be about the far distant future, we now plan our weekend around our yard work and errands or kids' soccer games and dance rehearsals. It's easy to think the problem is the choices we've made—we got the wrong job, the wrong house, or the wrong friends.

But it may just be that we've lost our ability to see. We no longer perceive the magic around us. The once-active imagination now sputters and stalls. The problem isn't the house or the job or the friends or our kids' activities. The problem is we've lost a *holy imagination*.

This is not how the people of God used to see the world. The Hebrew poets and prophets talked about the relationship between God and His world like this:

The earth is the LORD's and the fullness thereof,
  the world and those who dwell therein,

for he has founded it upon the seas
and established it upon the rivers. (Psalm 24:1–2)

Be exalted, O God, above the heavens!
Let your glory be over all the earth! (Psalm 57:5)

And one called to another and said:
"Holy, holy, holy is the LORD of hosts;
the whole earth is full of his glory!" (Isaiah 6:3)

The whole earth is full of God's glory. God, the holy God, the God who is above and beyond everything and everyone else—*His* glory is filling not only the *heavens* but also *the earth*!

Think about that for a minute. When we speak about God's holiness, we tend to emphasize His distance from us. To be holy is to be *different from* and completely *other than* anything else. That is true—the Hebrew notion of holiness is a kind of separateness from everything else. It is, in one sense, the very opposite of commonness. But this otherness is not all that is true of God. What Isaiah saw was something more radical than we imagine: God is holy *and* His glory fills the earth. God is not only above and beyond His creation; He is also somehow within it. God is holy, and He is filling the common with glory. The heavens are open above the earth.

Long before the prophet Isaiah penned those words, a herdsman named Jacob had a dream of the heavens opening up. He was on the run, embarrassed about his deception and afraid for his life. He had just fooled his father into blessing him instead of his brother, Esau, with a blessing reserved for firstborn sons. The blessing was a practice that had come to symbolize a life trajectory, a sense of destiny. And so here was Jacob, on the run with a stolen destiny, wondering what lay before him (see Genesis 28).

As Jacob lay his head down that night to what could only have been a troubled sleep, he found a stone to use as a pillow. One would not guess that these would be the conditions suitable to pleasant dreams. Yet even as a man running for his life, he dreamed while he slept.

He saw the heavens open up and angels ascending and descending in that place. And he heard the voice of the Lord say to him, "I am the LORD, the God of Abraham your father and the God of Isaac" (verse 13). Immediately, God identified Himself as the God of Jacob's grandfather and father.

With this identification God reminded Jacob that he had not cut himself off from that lineage or that heritage. And then God spoke to him about his destiny and the promise that had been given to his family: "The land on which you lie I will give to you and to your offspring. Your offspring shall be like the dust of the earth, and you shall spread abroad to the west and to the east and to the north and to the south, and in you and your offspring shall all the families of the earth be blessed" (verses 13–14). The promise was still in effect.

Then came a promise just for Jacob: "Behold, I am with you and will keep you wherever you go, and will bring you back to this land. For I will not leave you until I have done what I have promised you" (verse 15). It was personal. God was not simply honoring a promise to his grandfather; God would be present to Jacob.

Jacob woke up and said what may be the truest words he had ever spoken: "Surely the LORD is in this place, and I did not know it" (verse 16).

This is the description of a world beginning to awaken to the nearness of God. We are all Jacob. We scheme to enhance our futures and fortunes because we think no one out there is watching over us. We stretch the truth and manipulate the outcomes because who knows if there's a God or not? Even if there is one, He's too far away or too preoccupied to notice. If there is a heaven, it's way out there somewhere.

But then we glimpse something. It may not be a dream or a heavenly vision. It may simply be a spark, a surge of joy, or a flash of awe. We bump against the mystery and wonder of it all. Our imaginations are awakened. And we see it: *God* is here. God has been here the whole time. The heavens are open. The whole earth is *full* of His glory.

That's not just the sun signaling the start of a new day; it's the witness of the steadfast love of God that will always break the darkness of night. That's not just a dinner with friends; it's the music of laughter reminding us we're not alone. That's not just the sound of a baby crying in the night and robbing us of sleep; it's the evidence that your child is loved, that she believes you will care for her. These are all gifts from God, ordinary yet extraordinary, earthy yet filled with glory.

Sure, things can be reduced to technical descriptions and itemized particles, just as a great symphony can be explained as a mathematical sequence of sonic intervals. But music is more than math, and life is more than a sum of its events. In each moment, in each breath and thought and act, something more is going on. It is not merely ordinary.

Surely the Lord is in this place—the place where we are right now—and we do not know it.

It's true: the whole earth is full of His glory.

THE ONE WHO WATCHES OVER US

The sea was calm that night. A cool breeze came off the water and swept over me as I reclined in a wooden chair. I stared up into the starless sky, listening for the voice of the Lord. I would soon be boarding a plane to come to America by myself. I was seventeen.

That would be my second time moving to the States. The first was seven years earlier, when my parents obeyed the call of the Lord to leave their well-paying jobs and attend a Bible college in Portland, Oregon. My sister was thirteen, and I was ten. We thought the whole thing sounded like an adventure. "Move to America? Let's do it!" Our three years in the Pacific Northwest were special and full of wonderful memories: the international students at the Bible college, the rich times of worship and prayer at the church connected to it, and all the much-anticipated quintessential American experiences like eating pizza, camping, and playing schoolyard football.

But this time was different. It wouldn't be our whole family flying across the Pacific; it would just be me. I had watched a few years earlier as my sister went to America for college. She had come home for the summer, and we were on our last vacation together as a family—at a beautiful island resort in Malaysia, courtesy of a generous friend of my father's. Soon it would be my turn. Soon it would be time for me to fly to the other side of the world. At seventeen.

Yet, as I sat in that chair by the calm sea, I felt peace. It came like the gentle waves lapping onto the shore. It was a sense of God's presence with me, His nearness to me. He was there, even in that moment.

Some twenty years later I found myself in a similar place. This time sitting not on a beach but on a train in the middle of the English countryside, heading north from London to Durham. I had begun pursuing a doctorate in theology and ministry from Durham University. It was a desire that had been in my heart for a while, and my wife, Holly, encouraged me to go for the "dream option"— to study in the UK. I found a program that required only a few trips over there per year. Holly was a champ throughout the whole process, holding down the fort at home with our four kids. My parents, who had moved from Malaysia to America as I was beginning my doctoral studies, were also a tremendous help.

So there I was, across an ocean from my family, on my own again.

And it all just hit me. The loneliness. The ache. The fear. But also the peace.

It wasn't quite out of nowhere. I had worship music playing in my headphones, and I was reading *Harry Potter and the Prisoner of Azkaban*. It was my first time reading the Harry Potter books, and it felt only right since I was in the homeland of author J. K. Rowling—and on a train that had departed from King's Cross station en route to a place where some of the movies had been filmed!

I had initially begun reading the books to see if our oldest child, then around ten, should read them. I got hooked. The Harry Potter books employ a device known in fantasy fiction writing as incantational magic, as opposed to invocational magic. It is not a magic summoned from beyond the world, invoked from a supernatural beyond. It is a magic that is already present; the world in these sorts of stories is already enchanted. One merely needs to learn how to sing along. (This is what an incantation means.) Rowling, like J. R. R. Tolkien and C. S. Lewis and so many others before, created a world that is alive with a song, enchanted by a melody; goodness means singing along, and evil is a distortion of the tune.

The third Harry Potter book explores Harry's own longing for his father or for a father figure. Orphaned as a baby and raised by an aunt and uncle who despise him while spoiling their only child, Harry found a family at Hogwarts, the school for those gifted with magical abilities. The headmaster, Dumbledore, is a sort of fatherly figure but functions more as a sage grandfather. In the third book we are introduced to dementors, ghastly creatures that feed off people's fears and suck out all their joy. The only way to prevent them from doing so is to learn a patronus charm. Rowling chose her words on purpose. The term is an intentional play on the Latin word for a father—*pater*—from which we also get the word for one who supports a project or an artist—*patron*.

Moreover, the phrase the young students must recite to get their patronus—a magical creature who defends them against dementors—is *expecto patronum,* which roughly translates to, "I wait for a guardian." I like to think the phrase echoes the deep biblical longing "Deliver us!"

Harry struggles to summon a patronus, perhaps because he has so few happy memories—the fuel for making the charm work—or perhaps because he has had so few guardians and defenders. Finally, in the face of certain death as a swarm of dementors approach him, a patronus appears and saves him. But it comes from across a lake. Harry thinks it is his father from beyond the grave coming to save him. As it turns out—spoiler alert—it is Harry himself using the aid of a time turner. Yet in a strange way, it is Harry's belief that his father was watching out for him that gave him the strength to summon the patronus. I could be completely misreading the message, but that's my theory.

When I read that, I set the book down on the train's tray table in front of me and stared out the window. The worship music played on in my ears. I sensed a whisper deep in my soul. *I am with you. I have always been with you. I am watching over you, covering you, protecting you. No attack of the Enemy will prevail. I've got you.* That's what I heard in my heart. My Father in heaven was watching me.

Maybe I was imagining it. Or maybe I was seeing something that had been there all along. If *the whole earth is full of His glory,* if His glory is present with us rather than far away, it makes sense that we have this covering. We have the joy and holy confidence of walking with a present Guardian.

God has been with me . . . in the trip across the Pacific Ocean to go to college in America by myself and in the adventure across the Atlantic to pursue my doctorate. And in all the journeys in between. With others and by myself. In joys and in sorrows. In the spectacular and in the ordinary. *Surely the Lord is in this place* even when I did not know it.

There are moments when it can feel as if life is just carrying you along, like a plane flying over the ocean or a train hurtling through the countryside. You feel alone and far removed from everyone else. Why does it seem like you're the only one who doesn't have it all together? Why does it seem like everyone else is driving her own destiny but you seem to just be along for the ride? Why do the days and weeks seem to speed past like the blurred trees outside a train window while you're sitting idle? Life is just one more morning arriving with the sound of a phone alarm, one more day consumed at your desk, one more evening of scrounging around the kitchen for dinner.

These are the moments of quiet desperation, when the dull ache of loneliness makes the mundane unbearable.

But what if you could catch a glimpse? What if you let your imagination wander and your heart wake up with sight? What if you could see who's been there all along, the God who has always been present?

Your Protector, Deliverer, and Redeemer is watching over you. He is there when you wake, with you as you walk and work. He weeps with you when your heart is breaking; He sings over you when you've lost your words; He sits with you in the stillness. Surely the Lord is in your kitchen and in your car and in your office and in the moments of each day, though you do not know it. Yet.

SACRAMENTAL SEEING

One of the reasons we have such trouble seeing—truly seeing—is that we've been shaped by centuries of cultural tides that have taught us not to see, in fact, not to even look for anything beyond.

The Enlightenment was an era of thought that lasted roughly from the late 1600s through the early 1800s and was marked by philosophers and political theorists who saw the world as separated into two realms—the natural and the supernatural. The Enlightenment emerged on the shoulders of the scientific revolution, when new discoveries and advances were creating a sense of optimism about what humans could accomplish. It's always tricky to make blanket statements about somewhat arbitrarily drawn eras of history, but for much of the Western world, the Enlightenment drastically changed the way people saw the world. Instead of a *creation* in which the Creator was present and active, there was just *nature*. God was relegated "upstairs" to the supernatural realm, while humans inhabited the "downstairs" natural realm.

What emerged over time was a stripped-down version of Christianity that is more accurately called Deism. This belief system accepted that the order in creation owed its origins to a creator, but that like any good invention, it did not require its inventor to keep running. This eventually gave way to a rejection of miracles both in Scripture and in contemporary life. After all, why would God make rules only to suspend them whenever He liked? Why set the world up like a great clock only to move the hands at a whim? And if interventions were needed to correct the mechanism, how good was its design to begin with?

The truth is, the residual effects of this kind of thinking are still with us, even though we would never claim to be deists. We freely admit our need for God when it comes to spiritual matters such as the forgiveness of sin or the avoidance of hell. But for everything else, we'd rather be at the wheel. *Fine, God may have set up the rules and ordered the world, but I can take it from here.* Or maybe you've thought you *had* to take it from here because God is too busy, far away, or unconcerned to really care. You've been disappointed by His silence, so you've learned to go it alone. Whatever the reason, we move through each day like practical deists, like people who believe in God but have never thought to look for Him in the everyday moments. *Oh sure, there's a God, and I believe in Him. But what does that have to do with my job or my relationships or my money?*

For those who do look for God in the midst of life, faith can sometimes be used as an escape hatch from the boring realities of life. God is a means of transcendence, far above the unimportant, normal stuff. *Why bother about eating dinner with my family when I could go to another prayer meeting? Who cares about my silly job—I just need to listen to more worship music!*

These two extremes—being practical deists or spiritual escapists—are the remnants of warring worldviews. We now falsely assume that things are either/or. They are either common or holy, ordinary or sacred, material or spiritual.

Take, for example, the way we think about miracles. We tend to think of a miracle as God overriding the laws of nature, suspending the machine He built and set into motion, making an exception *just this once.* We have been conditioned to divide the world into physical and spiritual, natural and supernatural. Maybe God will once in a while override the natural and do something supernatural, but surely that's rare. Most of us live without ever witnessing such an event. Thus we make our peace with being ordinary.

But what if dividing reality into natural and supernatural is not only poor theology but also outmoded science? My doctoral supervisor, David Wilkinson, is a theologian and an astrophysicist. In a *Christian Today* interview on miracles and science, Wilkinson described how quantum theory reveals that the structure of the world in its smallest bits (not a technical term) is nothing like a mechanical clock. "It is a world," Wilkinson said, "that is unpicturable, uncertain, and in which the cause of events cannot be fully specified." In other words, there is room for God to act, move, and do the unexpected, precisely because the world is not a closed system, like a machine would be. The writer of the article summarized Wilkinson, saying, "He [God] can 'push' electrons here and there and alter the course of events in the world without breaking any of the laws of nature."[1]

This means that miracles are not God *overriding* the laws of the universe; they are signs of God at work *within* His world. (I can hear Jacob whispering again, "Surely the LORD is in this place, and I did not know it.")

There is a word for this view of the world: *sacramental.* That may conjure images of medieval superstition, or it may just add to the confusion. But a sacrament, as the fifth-century theologian Saint Augustine explained it, is an "outward, visible sign of an inward, invisible grace."[2] It is God making Himself known, making His presence felt. It is God opening our eyes to catch a glimpse of His abounding grace.

Two of the practices that are most widely held as sacraments in the church, regardless of denomination, are baptism and communion. Both practices focus not on what we are doing but on what God in Christ has done for us and what God through His Spirit is doing in us. At baptism the grace of God marks us as God's own. The waters speak of a new birth—being born of the Spirit. We are children of God, chosen and adopted. The Lord's Table reveals God's love for us through the body and blood of Jesus Christ. He died that we might live; His body was given that we might be whole; He bled that we might be cleansed. Sacraments reveal the glory of God's grace.

To be sacramental is to begin to see all God's gifts and handiwork as icons of His glory and grace. Look at the stars: they show us that even in darkness there is hope. Look at children: they remind us of what matters most. Look at bread: it reveals how wheat plucked from a field and placed in heat becomes something that nourishes life. God takes what appears to be common and makes it a conduit of glory.

Sacramental theology invites us to see the visible as a sign of the invisible, to believe that the common can be a carrier of the holy. Because God made this world, it is capable of being a container for His glory. The common can become sacred not because of a magical invocation that changes it but because this is what creation was made to be. The whole world is full of God's glory! And God has hidden His glory in the ordinary.

Your Life Is "Bread" in Jesus's Hands

Every time Jesus took bread in His hands, He did the same few things. He took it, blessed it, broke it, and gave it. Luke, more than the other gospel writers, made a point to use the same words every time: *blessed, broken, given.* The book in your hands is about those three words and how they can reshape the way we see our lives.

Jesus took bread, blessed it by giving thanks to the Father, broke it, and gave it. Bread in the hands of Jesus is *blessed, broken,* and *given.* And so it is with you. Your life, as common and ordinary as bread, in Jesus's hands becomes something more.

In the hands of Jesus, your life becomes *blessed.* This blessedness is not about accumulating or achieving more. Blessedness is about having your true identity recovered and your true calling revealed. It is to be given a new name. Once you were a sinner; now you are a saint. Once you were far off; now you are a cherished family member.

In the hands of Jesus, your life becomes *broken* in a new way. When you place the brokenness of your failure, frailty, and suffering in Jesus's hands, you become open to the grace of God. This brokenness is not about wallowing in your sin or fixating on how miserable you are. To be broken is to allow the grace of God to humble you, to lead you into vulnerability with others, and to transform your heart. After all, bread that is not broken cannot be shared.

In the hands of Jesus, your life becomes *given.* You realize you are not here for yourself. Life with Jesus is deeply personal but never private. The openness that comes from being broken is meant to lead you outward. There is a hunger in the world around us, a deep groan for something more. When your life becomes blessed and broken in Jesus's hands, He gives *you* out for the life of the world. You become the way others find the Bread of Life. But to be that way, you must first experience the blessing and embrace the brokenness—only then will you be consecrated to bring change in powerful ways.

Some scholars believe that these three movements became the shape of early Christian worship. For that reason the third chapter of each movement of this book focuses on what it looks like to live it out in the community of faith. What does it mean to be blessed together, to be broken with and for one another, to be given for one another?

We may have wondered, *Is there anything more* ordinary *than bread?* Now we see it: *Is there anything more* glorious *than bread?*

COME, CREATOR SPIRIT

In the pages ahead you will discover what happens when you awake from resignation, when you surrender your frenzy, when you turn over your failures and disappointments, placing your life in Jesus's hands. You'll discover what happens when you realize that the common can become sacred, that the material is not cut off from the spiritual, that the stuff of everyday life was made to be a container for glory.

The nineteenth-century English poet Gerard Manley Hopkins captured the wonder of this in his famous poem "God's Grandeur." He wrote that the world emanates God's splendor, but the human race keeps working without ever stopping to worship. People are busy with the daily grind, and the world bears the stains and scars from it. The soil is holy ground, but our feet are covered. And yet the closing lines of the final stanza haunt with beauty:

Because the Holy Ghost over the bent
World broods with warm breast and with ah! Bright wings.[3]

Imagine it: the Holy Spirit, the One who was brooding over
the primordial waters of chaos in the beginning, hovers over each
predawn blackness, waiting to breathe life again into the world.

And into you. Even now, the Spirit hovers over you. Welcome
Him. Let Him open your eyes to truly see. Let Him open your
ears to truly hear. The Spirit of God is the glory that fills the earth.
He is how God is in *this* place even when we do not know it. The
Spirit is how oil and water and bread become portals for the presence of God. The Spirit is how the ordinary and the extraordinary,
the natural and the supernatural, come together in the sacramental. One of oldest Christian confessions calls the Spirit the "Lord,
the Giver of Life." The same Holy Spirit who filled up the world
with life fills all who are in Christ. And because of that, nothing
about your life is *merely ordinary.*

The ancient prayer of the church beckons Him: *Veni Creator
Spiritus*—"Come, Creator Spirit":

Come, Holy Ghost, Creator, come
from thy bright heav'nly throne;
come, take possession of our souls,
and make them all thine own.[4]

So we pray, "Come, Creator Spirit." We are ready to surrender, to return our lives to the Lord, to go back to the beginning
so that we can begin with God. We come to place our lives—

our common and ordinary days, our imperfect and inadequate selves—fully in Jesus's hands. These are the hands of the One who is "the image of the invisible God," the One by whom "all things were created, in heaven and on earth, visible and invisible," the One through whom and for whom "all things were created," the One who is "before all things," the One in whom "all things hold together" (Colossians 1:15–17).

Everything begins here.

BLESSED

2

Origins

What does it mean to be blessed? The word *blessed* implies that something has been bestowed upon us by a divine being. It emerges from the lexicon of faith. People who believe in a god—usually a sort of benevolent god—use a word like *blessed*.

But if a sociologist with no religious background came to our community to learn the word's meaning solely by its usage on social media, he might develop a very different understanding of the word.

To be #Blessed is to be living the good life, to have things work out just the way you want. It is having your favorite artisan coffee shop a short walk from your new apartment or getting a promotion at work or finding a boyfriend or girlfriend who seems to be right out of a magazine shoot. It's a vacation at the most Instagramable location or a Pinterest-worthy kitchen remodel. In short, it is to be living the dream.

Let me say there's nothing inherently wrong with seeing these things as blessings from God. It's a little like people who pray for prime parking spots. I used to consider this a petty, self-consumed, #FirstWorldProblems kind of thing. But now I think I may have misjudged the situation. Maybe people are just trying to practice the habit of turning to God in all things. Maybe it's a way to live with gratitude before God for the small things. And so in a similar way, maybe considering these daily fortunes as flowing from God's hand is just another way of counting our blessings.

That's true, insofar as it goes. And for the most part, it's harmless.

But we start to run into problems when these material blessings of comfort and convenience are seen not as *hints* of a blessed life but rather as the *essence* of one. It's one thing to thank God for the little things, even the seemingly trivial successes; it's another thing altogether to assume that blessing equates to a happily-ever-after, perfectly charmed life. When we think about blessing in this manner, we miss the beauty, wonder, and majesty of many blessings that we're already participating in.

Not surprisingly, we have no clue what to do with suffering and hardship. What happens when things *don't* go as planned? What happens when the job is given to someone else, when the doctor's report isn't positive, when the house doesn't sell, when the relationship or marriage ends? Are we still blessed? Does this mean that God has pulled His blessing from our lives?

I want you to see a bigger picture of what it means to be blessed. I want to lead you to a bedrock of blessedness that won't be shaken when storms come hurtling your way. There will be days when things don't work out as you had hoped. Sometimes trouble will come *because* of your obedience to Christ; sometimes trouble will come *despite* it. But the truth is, we are blessed even when our lives are not Instagram worthy. We are blessed even when our lives don't appear to look like someone else's blessed life. We are blessed even when it seems everything in our lives is falling apart.

How can this be?

Because being blessed is deeper, richer, and more fulfilling than being #Blessed. Being #Blessed is about the superficial and the circumstantial. Being blessed the way the Scriptures describe it is about something more, something that has to do with the very core of who we are and how we were made. And to understand that, we need someone else to tell us our own story.

TELL ME WHAT I WAS LIKE

Standing over the plastic drawer-like crib resting on a metal cart, I began to weep. My parents were beside me, and my wife reclined on the hospital bed behind me. It had been a relatively short labor, and now she was here—our first child, our daughter, Sophia, swaddled in this unspectacular hospital cradle.

Of all the miracles in the world, of all the signs of God at work within the fabric of the cosmos, your child's entry into the world is surely among the most stunning. Birth is a beginning. Yes, life begins in the womb, but as a dad I was not privy to the growth and movements of this miraculous child until she exited the womb and entered the world.

Standing there next to the people who brought me into the world, it hit me: life is continuing; a generation of our family has been added. The story goes on.

I wept.

With the birth of each of our four children, Holly and I felt waves of emotion. Every few seconds in the world, a child is born, and yet every time it is a miracle. And every time we see the miracle, we are witnesses to the start of a story, the beginning of a journey. And the crazy thing about it is that the baby is unable to absorb the moment or even remember it. Parents play a huge role in shaping their children's awareness of their early experiences by the stories they tell them. It takes someone else to tell a child her story.

Once in a while Holly and I will pull out a photo book depicting the first five years of one of our children's lives. The child featured in the book will invariably say, "Tell me what I was like as a baby." Then Holly will recount the child's sleep patterns (or lack thereof!) and food preferences and what made this child giggle or cry. I chime in with the silly rituals I engaged in to get him to sleep or what stories she liked. It's uncanny how many little seeds of their personalities—now in fuller bloom for our older two, who are teenagers—were there even when they were babies and toddlers.

When a child asks a parent, "Tell me what I was like . . ." it may well be a way of saying, "Remind me who I am." Identity has a beginning; destiny has an origin.

One of the more brilliant bits of parenting advice we received was to keep a journal for each child. Over the years Holly and I have recorded our children's likes and dislikes, quirks and idiosyncrasies, and memorable one-liners and retorts. There were far more entries in their early years. But even as they've gotten older, we have made it a point of writing in the journals at least twice a year. At some point the entries became less like note taking and more like letters. We address the children personally, describing what we see in them and how we see God at work in their young lives.

They know these journals exist, but they don't quite know what's in them, and they know they are not to reach for them on the bookshelf. (So far, so good.) When our oldest, Sophia, turned thirteen, we presented the journal to her to read for the first time. We let her read the notes and letters we've been writing about her since she was born. She was mesmerized. For much of her birthday, her head was buried in the pages of the journal. All the while she would smile and giggle and call out quotes to the rest of us. Sophia had been given the gift of knowing a crucial part of her own story; she could see the origins of her identity. We will continue to write in the journal until she's eighteen, and then it will be hers to keep. But we knew that these next years will be crucial for her as a cacophony of voices will bombard her, each one trying to tell her who she is. We want the Lord to be the voice that shapes her. So we are trying to use our voices as parents to echo His.

This, I think, is a picture of what it means to be blessed. It is to be taken back to the start, to have Father God show us what He saw in us when He made us. In fact, what we have been given in the Bible is even wider than that: it is God's account of the story of the world, from the very beginning.

GOD SAW THAT IT WAS GOOD

Our origin story is rooted in the origin story of the whole cosmos. God established blessing from the origins and foundations of the world. If we want to understand who we are and what makes us blessed, we have to go back to the creating, ordering, and blessing of the world.

When the Bible tells us the story of the beginning, it begins with a person, God. "In the beginning, God . . ." (Genesis 1:1). All things have their origin in God. In the ancient world everyone knew that *some* god or collection of gods was responsible for the material world. They were not like people in our day, who imagine the world as a series of automated processes or random incidents with no divine involvement. For people in ancient times, the questions were not "Did God make this?" and "How?" but rather "Which god made this?" and "Why?" The questions of which god and why are massively significant, and these are the ones the Genesis account wants to answer most clearly.

To illuminate the picture of God presented in Genesis, we need to set the backdrop. Like an artist working with vivid contrasts to make a subject stand out, God reveals Himself in the Scriptures in a way that is especially stunning against the landscape of other origin stories from the ancient Middle East. I'll describe just two.

First: The ancient Sumerians living around 3000 BC had two traditions that appear in a few of their sacred texts. In one, the god An, representative of heaven, is united with the goddess Antum or Ki, representative of earth. Their union fertilizes the earth, causing life—humans, animals, vegetation—to spring up and flourish. In the other tradition, Enki, the god of fertility, produces a spring that carries life to the earth through streams and rivers, with life springing up around it. In both of these Sumerian traditions, humans were created "to serve the gods, to save them from having to work."[1]

Second: Perhaps the best-known ancient cosmology, besides

the Genesis account, is the *Enuma Elish*. This Akkadian account (with copies dating from 1100 BC) was reproduced numerous times and was often recited at the New Year festival.[2] The story is lengthy and bloody but is essentially a power struggle among the gods, driven by jealousy and anger. The god Marduk becomes greater than his divine predecessors. Though at first this provokes the jealousy of the other gods, he strikes a deal with them: he will fight on their behalf if they give him the power of "fixing destinies."[3] They agree. Marduk kills Tiamat, splitting her body in two, one half becoming the sky and the other half becoming the earth. Marduk orders that Ea make humans out of the blood of Kingu, the leader of the rebel gods. Like the Sumerians, the Babylonians believed humans were created to serve and work for the gods.

To the question "Which god made the heavens and the earth?" many of Israel's ancient neighbors would answer with names of regional gods who were power hungry and jealous, making deals to gain more jurisdiction and stopping at nothing—even murder—to rule over all.

To the question "Why did they make humans?" the answer would be that humans were made to be slaves of the gods—to do work the gods didn't want to do.

This is *not* very good news.

When you start to compare the Genesis account to the other ancient accounts, you see how Scripture reveals a different kind of God. In particular, notice three things that set the God of Genesis apart from the gods of the day.

First, Genesis reveals that there is *only one God*. He is the supreme, sovereign God. Genesis reveals an entirely unique view of the spiritual realm. In contrast to the many other ancient Middle Eastern beliefs, one God stands apart as the sole sovereign ruler over all creation: YHWH (the Hebrew rendering of Yahweh, or God). Genesis depicts no division of divine jurisdiction. Unlike the way their neighbors thought, Israelites did not have a separate god of the sea, god of the land, or god of fertility. There was and is only one God. The primacy of God must have been striking to a young Israelite child hearing these stories for the first time. And it must have been captivating to hear the famous words repeated at holy assemblies: "Hear, O Israel: the LORD our God, the LORD is one" (Deuteronomy 6:4). YHWH is set apart as uniquely powerful, greater than all other gods.

As the lead character in the opening scenes, God not only exists but also acts. God is all through the opening passage as the only active character. There are no rivals and no one else adding input or ideas. There is simply God, who speaks, forms, makes, calls, and blesses.

The second thing that is different from other ancient accounts is that the sole sovereign God creates the world *on purpose* and *with purpose*. While that might seem obvious to us, it was not for ancient readers. As we noted previously, some ancient beliefs saw creation as the result of a bloody battle among the gods, the result of mutated divine excretions, or the gods' way of getting cheap labor around the universe.

The God of Genesis, however, sets out to make the world carefully, deliberately, methodically, and even poetically. The opening chapter of Genesis has a songlike cadence to it. Genesis 1 and 2 were meant to be a purpose story, a song about why we're here and why it matters. And just what does Genesis say about why we're here? It tells us we are here because God called us into being. God made us on purpose and with a purpose in mind. Not for cosmic labor but for divine relationship.

The third thing that stands out in contrast to the other origin stories is that God *blesses* what He makes. Not only is God the sole sovereign and an intentional creator, but He is also the God who loves and blesses what He creates.

From the beginning the God who creates blesses what He has made. And why wouldn't He? After all, He meant to make it. He called it good. The word *good* has many meanings, but in some usage it has resonances with what we might call "beautiful." In a very real way, all that is good and beautiful in the world is the result of God's blessing.

Imagine the people of God living in exile in Babylon, not feeling very #Blessed. They strain their eyes to see something of God's hand and train their ears to hear something of God's voice, when all of a sudden they remember: *This world was made by God!* This tree, this stream, this flower, this fruit—everything that flourishes around them—flourishes because God has *blessed* it. The blessing of God on the material world would have been a source of consolation and a spark of worship in an otherwise difficult land of exile.

Maybe they remembered it most when they took bread and gathered the whole household around the table to pray. "Blessed art Thou, LORD our God, King of the universe, who brings forth bread from the earth . . ."[4] This is how the Hebrew meal prayer begins—by blessing the God who is *their* God, who is the *sovereign* God, who is the God who gives them *bread*. And with that common yet glorious bread, the people of God remembered: God makes everything on purpose and for a purpose. God calls even the simple and ordinary and material good.

And because He says so, it is so. Good and beautiful.

The Origins of You

Good and beautiful. Is that how you see yourself? Maybe on a good day. But we often struggle to see ourselves as good *or* beautiful, let alone both. We're too aware of our shortcomings or our plainness. *I'm not really good; I'm a bit of a mess, actually. And beautiful? Well, I wouldn't say that. Maybe just ordinary.*

The Genesis story grounds us in God. God Himself made us on purpose and for a purpose and blessed us by calling us good and beautiful. That is our origin story. But Genesis also gives us the origin of sin, the way the world began to unravel. We're not wrong in our instinctive sense that we are somehow less than what we should be. Christians have called Genesis 3 the story of the Fall—the way humans fell "short of the glory of God" (Romans 3:23). For so many of us, our understanding of the gospel begins there, with our fallenness. *We were messed up; we were sinners; we were failures . . . but God loved us anyway.* This makes us feel very good about God but pretty lousy about ourselves. And we even secretly wonder if God isn't just tolerating us anyway.

But if you go back to the beginning, to the origin story of you, of the world, of all humanity, you realize that the Fall is not the start of the story. Sin is not the opening line. Blessedness is our beginning. Sin is what mars the image, what turns the soul inward, bending its desires into self-seeking drives. In various biblical passages we see that sin is like a stain, a sickness unto death, a power that enslaves. What you see in all those pictures is that sin is not the substance; it is the destruction of the substance. It is the deviation or subversion of something else: the good. Just as death is the negation of life, sin is the perversion of the good.

In the chapters to come, we will look more closely at how God takes the brokenness of our sin and returns us to the blessing. But for now I want you to see what God sees. When you're trying to figure out what God is doing in your life or why it matters or how it can be of value, don't look at your current state—go back to the beginning. The truest thing about you is not who you are now or what you have done; the truest thing about you is who God made you to be.

Salvation is God's way of setting things back on track, putting the world back together again, and making you who He made you to be.

It takes God to do that. No amount of self-talk or self-help or positive mantras will do the trick. That's why the word *blessed* is so important: it denotes an action being done to us by a being far above us. As Christians, we know that only God can bless. Only the Creator who called the world into existence and called it good can bless. Only the Creator can be the Redeemer. Only the God who once scanned the cosmos and called it good can rescue and redeem and return it to its goodness.

There is no need to try to make something of yourself. There is no need to cover up and pretend. There is no need to give yourself a makeover. If you let Him, He will take you back to the start, return you to your origin, bring you back to the moment He *blessed* you.

To be blessed is to be who we were originally made to be. And that blessing happens when we place ourselves in Jesus's hands. Like bread.

Jesus Took Bread and Blessed It

Every time Jesus took bread in the Gospels, He blessed it. In blessing it, He made it something more. But in another way, He was returning the bread to what it was made to be. The Orthodox theologian Alexander Schmemann reminds us of the power of God's original blessing, of what it means for God to bless His world: "God *blesses* everything He creates, and, in biblical language, this means that He makes all creation the sign and the means of His presence and wisdom, love and revelation."[5]

At Passover Jesus took bread and blessed it in an extraordinary way. He called it His body. For all the things that phrase could mean, at the very least it means that coming to the Lord's Table and receiving communion is a moment to experience the presence of God.

For the first few centuries of Christian worship, theologians spent little energy on answering the question of *how* God was present at the Table. It did not matter how the bread was also Christ's body. All that mattered was that somehow Christ was present to His church when they gathered at His Table. It was only later—during medieval times—that a group of theologians wanted to try to explain how. They began to propose that a change in the very substance of bread and wine was taking place. In other words, bread being bread and wine being wine was not *holy* enough. It needed to become something more. It needed to change in its very substance.

But the sacramental view, a much earlier Christian view, says that signs don't need to change in substance in order to signify something holy. Physical things like water and oil and bread and wine can serve as signs of something more without ceasing to be physical things. That's why Saint Augustine said that sacraments were an "outward, visible sign of an inward, invisible grace."[6] Signs don't need to change in substance in order to signify something holy. Bread doesn't need to change in substance to become sacred.

Why? Because bread is the fruit of the soil that God made and blessed and called good. In blessing the world, God made every part of His creation a *sign* and a *means* of His presence. Bread doesn't need to become something different than bread to be a *sign* of God's presence. That's precisely what bread was made to be! And bread doesn't need to be transformed into something else to be a *means* of God's presence. That's what bread and wine and the whole earth itself was made to be: a carrier of God's glory.

In blessing the bread, Jesus not only returned it to its origin but also pointed to its future, and not just the future of bread but also the future of the material world. The communion table is not just a place to remember the past—Christ's death on the cross—and to encounter the presence of the risen Christ through the Holy Spirit. It is also a place where we anticipate the future. At the Lord's Table we pray for eyes to see what bread will be when the new creation arrives in fullness. Bread, like everything in creation, will be filled with the glory of God. When heaven comes down to earth, when God makes His dwelling place with humankind, bread and wine and all of creation will become what it was made to be. The ending shall complete the beginning. So in blessing the bread, Jesus pointed to the *origin* and to the *destiny* of creation.

Why am I telling you all this? Because I suspect we're not far off from medieval thinking. We subconsciously believe we must become something other than what we are in our very essence in order to be sacred. We become convinced—deep down in our bones—that our substance is not good enough, not holy enough, not special enough to matter. That's not true.

Maybe your story is one of pain. Maybe your beginnings, as far as you can tell, are pretty messed up or unspectacular. Maybe you've thought that there's not much of a future for you. If the starting point wasn't special, how could it lead to an ending that is? I'm here to tell you there's a bigger story. It's a story of a God who made you on purpose and for a purpose, who took pleasure in you. He wants to recover your identity. He wants to reveal your purpose. He wants to *bless* you.

So come. Place your life like bread in Jesus's hands. Only Jesus can return us to our origin. Only Jesus can carry us to our destiny. Jesus is the author and the finisher of our faith.

When God Calls You Blessed

Can you hear it now?

The God who called the cosmos into being, who called the stars into order and the seas to their limits on the shores . . .

The God who called Abraham out of his father's house, who called Moses out of hiding and Israel out of Egypt . . .

The God who called David from the valley and called His people out of exile . . .

The God who called Mary blessed among women . . .

The God who called Jesus out of the waters of baptism "Beloved Son" . . .

The God who called fishermen and tax collectors to be disciples of His Son . . .

The God who called Jesus out of the tomb and into resurrection life . . .

The God who called a church together from the uttermost parts of the earth and filled it with His Spirit . . .

This God—Father, Son, and Holy Spirit—is calling *you*.

And God calls you blessed.

Being blessed is not a state—it's a story. It's an origin story. It's the story of how you began and why. It's the story of God the creator calling you into being on purpose and for a purpose. It's the story of God taking delight in you and naming you as good and beautiful. It's the story of God the redeemer pursuing you, calling you, and returning you to who He made you to be. The God who called light out of darkness calls you out of darkness and into light. In doing so, He brings you back to the beginning, to *your* beginning. This is where it starts:

You are blessed.

3

Names

A parent's power to shape a child's life begins with a simple act: naming her. A name, at the very least, determines what the child will be called. The most recognizable word in any language is our own name. We pick it out in a crowd; we hear it in a whisper. It can even awaken us from deep slumber. Just the sound of our name. Think of it: something so powerful, so personal, so intimate as our own name, and we didn't even have any say in what it would be.

For many cultures, a name is not just what you are called but who you will be. A name carries with it a sense of identity and even destiny. The Puritans who came to America seemed to take such an approach. The log of passengers aboard the *Mayflower* included names like "Humility Cooper" and "Resolved White."[1] The next generation of Puritans, perhaps in an effort to one-up their parents, moved beyond the one-word virtues and opted for something more like a pep-talk slogan. There was "Fight-the-Good-Fight-of-Faith Wilson" and "Kill-Sin Pemble." But my favorites are the ones that serve as lifelong instruction from the parents, called to mind every time the names were spoken, such as "Be-Courteous Cole."

These sorts of names were rare—fewer than 4 percent of Puritan children bore these unconventional names. But still, you have to admire the boldness of those parents who said, "Well, honey, if we get the awesome privilege of shaping our child's destiny by bestowing a name, then by golly, let's give 'im a good one."

But the story of names in America has a dark side. Many immigrants from non-English speaking countries changed their names to better assimilate. Paul Revere's original family name—the one his father bore—was Rivoire. Paul's father, Apollos Rivoire, was a French Huguenot refugee.[2] Changing your name to aid pronunciation is one thing; changing it to avoid persecution is another. For Jewish immigrants a blatantly Jewish name could have been a barrier to thriving in the wider society. Thus Israel Baline became Irving Berlin, and Nathan Birnbaum came to be known as George Burns.[3] The story is bleakest for those brought to America as slaves. Bought and sold as property, valued as only three-fifths of a person, these individuals carried no trace of their original identity. If named at all, they were given, tragically and ironically, Christian names, as if this were a kindness.

Names matter. Being named is personal, just as being de-named is depersonalizing.

What's in a name? In a word, *personhood*.

A New Name

When my father was born, he was named after a Hindu god as is customary in many Hindu families. Indra is described as a god who conquered evil, the one who overcame all that stands in the way of happiness and prosperity. He is the god of lightning and rain.

By the time I was born, my father had become a Christian. He had met my mother at the National University of Singapore, and they fell in love. But she told him she wouldn't marry a Hindu. While she didn't have a very active or personal faith, her family was Christian at least in name, and therefore she knew she wouldn't marry a Hindu. Her resolution was clear, so my dad converted.

Of course, the story is more complex than that. There were other things working in my dad's heart. People who study religious conversions tell us there is always a push (an event or situation that makes you want to leave your current religion) and a pull (something that makes you want to join a different one).[4] I don't know what the push was for my dad, but I know the pull was love—not just his love for the woman he wished to marry but also the love of Jesus.

Several years into their marriage, my dad experienced what many Christians call a born-again moment—a radical renewal of the heart and mind that results in a total surrender and commitment to follow Jesus. The best way for Dad to demonstrate this transformation was to change his name. As he read the Bible, he was drawn to an Old Testament character who was flawed but had a heart after God. And so it was that my dad would no longer be Indra; he would thereafter be called David.

Name changes are as old as Abram, the first person in the Bible to change his name. Except in Abram's case, it was God who gave him a new name. The difference between the name Abram and Abraham may seem slight, but the timing of the name change is every bit as significant as the added *ha* in the name. His name was changed as a sign of God's blessing.

For Abraham, the change marked a calling out of his father's house and a calling into the story of God launching His rescue mission. It was a calling to be the carrier of blessing to all the families of the earth. Abraham would be the beginning of a nation, and that nation would be the first of many God would add to his family. His blessing was to be the world's blessing.

All of this was marked by a name change.

And why shouldn't it be? To be blessed is to be renamed, to be given a new identity and a new purpose. It is to be re-storied.

That's what happened to Abram.

And that's what happened to Indra.

ORIGIN, DESTINY, AND NAMES

Maybe you grew up in a home where you were constantly called a nuisance or a pest or an idiot. Or maybe something worse. I remember cringing as a child when I would visit a schoolmate's home and hear one of his parents rail at him, calling him good for nothing, lazy, and stupid. This was not uncommon in Malaysia when a child brought home a bad report card or received a low score on an important exam. I saw good boys—boys who worked hard and tried their best—burst into tears at their parents' tirade. I saw young teens tremble when exam results were announced for fear of what awaited them when they got home. Grown men and women who were otherwise kind and upstanding members of society would unleash a cruel torrent of words toward their children, believing it would shake them to their senses and spur them toward success.

What I witnessed in the families around me growing up does

not even compare to more violent and damaging forms of abuse that many experience at an early age at the hands of parents or stepparents—people who are supposed to be protectors, guardians, stewards, and cultivators of our identity. The pain of their actions cannot be glossed over or easily resolved.

I don't know all the reasons parents say cruel things to their children. Addictions, mental health problems, stress, and wounds from their own childhood no doubt play significant roles. And even if empathy toward them were possible, it does not make their actions excusable. Nor does it remove the sting, the pain, or the wound inflicted on innocent children.

But there is a God who sees, who hears, who calls us by our true names.

What would it mean to recover the meaning and value God gave you? What would it be like to be returned to your true identity and purpose? It might not immediately remove the scars of your backstory, but it would invite you into a new and blessed story, one with a deeper beginning and a more glorious ending, one with new hope and a promise.

THE ONE WHO NAMED GOD

There is a kind of blessing that comes with being renamed by God. But there is another kind of blessing in seeing God so clearly that you name *Him*. A few chapters after the Bible introduces us to Abram, we meet a woman who experienced that second kind of blessing.

She was a slave. A female Egyptian slave. Nothing could have defined her more as an outsider. In her day she would have been considered the opposite of blessed. To be a female in the ancient world meant being regarded as valuable only insofar as you were useful . . . to a man. Whether for offspring or pleasure or domestic labor, a woman's usefulness was something she had to prove. She was thought to possess no intrinsic value.

To be Egyptian, in the eyes of Israelites, meant being an enemy. Later generations of Israelite children, listening to these stories of their heritage, would have marked this slave as belonging to the wrong group.

To be a slave meant having no freedom and no future. Slaves had no rights, no inheritance, no destiny.

If a name can create value, meaning, and destiny, then to be introduced in the biblical narrative as a female Egyptian slave was to signify that she had little value, a negative meaning, and no destiny. There is no reason we should know her name. She should be ancillary to the story, an outsider, invisible to God.

Except that God *knew her name.* And He called her by her name: Hagar.

In Genesis 16 we find Hagar on the run because Sarai, wife of the newly blessed Abraham, was jealous and resentful toward her. Sarai, unable to conceive and therefore unable to do her part in bringing about the promised blessing of offspring, gave her servant to her husband. This was not an uncommon practice in the ancient Middle East, but you don't need to be a psychologist to imagine the complicated emotions involved in such a choice, to say nothing of the swirl of feelings that result from it. Sarai perhaps resented Hagar for conceiving right away; she may have been jealous of Abraham's joy in a child she was unable to produce; she might have regretted her own actions. The Bible is clear that Sarai felt Hagar's contempt for her. Maybe Hagar, for the first time in her life, felt powerful. She could do something her master could not: bear a child.

But just as she was enjoying this newfound power and wondering if it might lead to a change of status, she began to be mistreated. Genesis says that Sarai was harsh with Hagar. Things had gotten so bad that she thought fleeing into the wilderness with no provisions and no plan would be better than staying in that house. Hagar, pregnant with Ishmael, was prepared to die in the desert.

Hagar thought it was over. She was sure no one would help and no one would come to her rescue.

But God did.

God found Hagar by a well in the wilderness. She had stopped at a spring for what could have been one last drink. And then an angel of the Lord met her there and called her *by her name*.

"Hagar, servant of Sarai, where have you come from and where are you going?" (Genesis 16:8). Yes, God was aware of her station in life, and He knew that she was a female Egyptian slave. He also knew her name.

And he asked her two questions: "Where have you come from and where are you going?"

When God asks a question, He's not launching an interrogation; He's staging an intervention. These two questions were about *origin* and *destiny*. Hagar thought she knew her origin and her destiny, where she had come from and where she was going. But God was about to rewrite her story.

God told Hagar to go back to Abraham's house, not because God condoned Sarai's mistreatment of her, but because there was no other way for Hagar to be saved. She would die in that wilderness. But in Abraham's house she would still be covered by the blessing. God's hand was on that household, and Hagar would benefit from it; she would be sustained and fed. And when the time came for her to leave, God would provide for her and her son in a new way.

For the time being, God wanted her to know there was a way for her to share in the blessing. She was not an outsider. She was not unnamed and unseen. He knew her name, and He saw her.

The angel said to Hagar, "I will surely multiply your offspring so that they cannot be numbered for multitude" (Genesis 16:10). Did you catch it? This was *Abraham's* blessing. This was the promise that was restated when God made a covenant with Abraham in the chapter right before the Hagar story—that his offspring would be like the stars, too many to count. Right from the start, God made it clear: He wants everyone to be able to get in on the blessing. He desires all to be swept up in his saving and redeeming love.

When Hagar understood this, she was in awe. She hadn't seen just a concept or an attribute of God—she had seen *God! This is what God is like!* Later, Moses would glimpse God and know that He is abounding in mercy and rich in love. But long before the great prophet Moses would see it, the female Egyptian slave Hagar saw it.

The angel went on. What would be the sign that God saw her

and heard her? The baby she was pregnant with was a son. And he was to be named Ishmael—which literally means "God hears." The angel said, "For the LORD has heard your cry of affliction" (Genesis 16:11, CSB).

Hagar responded to this blessing by blessing God. How? By *naming God*. "So she named the LORD who spoke to her: 'You are El-roi.'" Translated, this term means "God sees me." Hagar then said, "In this place, have I actually seen the one who sees me?" (verse 13, CSB).

Sometimes the blessing comes when God renames you. Sometimes the blessing comes in being able to see God's character so clearly that you can name *Him*. You can say what He is like because you have seen Him.

Pause here for a moment. Can you see God here with you, in the middle of your story, chasing after you in the wilderness of your soul?

God sees you. God hears your cry. God knows your name.

Forget the names you hear in your head. Never mind the other names you've been called or the ones you've called yourself. You are not an outsider. You are not unnamed and unseen.

God is rewriting your story, changing the way you answer the question of where you have come from and where you are going. The way your story began is not the way it will end. Your family of origin will not have the final say about who you are. Your current trajectory is not fixed, and your future is not predetermined.

Yes, your life will be a journey. No, it will not be easy.

But God has found you in the desert, and He wants you to know the blessing is for *you*.

BLESSING OTHERS

There's another layer to the Hagar story. We can see ourselves as Hagar on the run in the desert, chased down by God. But we can also see ourselves as the messengers of God who *find* the "Hagars" in the desert, who find those who are struggling and feeling like they have no hope.

There are Hagars in our world—in *your* world. They feel unnamed and unseen. They have experienced so much hurt that they think death may be a better option than a life full of pain. To make it worse, the people who know God and would be expected to show His mercy sometimes fail to treat others with mercy. Christians, who are supposed to be the ones blessed with the experience of God's grace, can at times be the least gracious people in the world. And so the ones who feel judged, hated, and excluded by Christians flee the church, the house of blessing.

If that's you, if this has been your experience—if you have felt judged and rejected by the very people who should have welcomed you with grace and mercy—I'm so sorry. As a pastor, as a priest, as a representative of the community of God's people, I'm sorry that the church, like Sarai, has been a source of pain and hurt. That should not be. It is wrong. For all the reasons you've left, for all the reasons you are on the run and have become spiritually homeless, I am so, so sorry.

My hope is that for every Hagar out there, an angel in the wilderness will remind her that even the people who carry the blessing are not the same as the God who blesses. People fail; God does not. People can be cruel; God is not. People can try to push you out into the wilderness; God is there to *bless you by your name.*

For some of us, the mission is to be the messenger in the desert, to be like that angel sent by God to Hagar. We can be the ambassadors, the representatives, who demonstrate God's nature up close to another human being. We can help the ones who are hurting to recover their value and their destiny. We can call them by their names. God still blesses by passing the blessing through His people.

Some of the most important work I do as a pastor is to *see* people, to really see them, wherever they are on their journey. Meeting after meeting, story after story, the conversation is never really about challenges at work or difficulties with family members or theological questions or ethical dilemmas. It is really about *where they have come from* and *where they are going.* And I am there to be a witness and to show them as best I can that God sees them, God hears them, and God knows their names.

Sometimes the conversations happen in the unlikeliest places. I was on a ministry trip halfway around the world when I realized an old friend might be in the same city. I reached out over social media, and sure enough, he was there. Somehow we both had the evening free, so we did a little sightseeing and then had a meal together.

Like bread that becomes more than bread, our conversation became more than just another meeting of friends. It was an occasion for blessing to pass between us. I hadn't realized the way our paths had run parallel over the previous few years. Though we live and work in mostly different spheres, our journeys and struggles of faith had many points of intersection. As we finished our meal and were getting ready to leave, I felt a nudge to tell him that he had done well, that his journey was important, that it had taught him much and was shaping him in all the right ways. It wasn't simply a validation; it was a blessing. I told him that he wasn't alone and that he wasn't crazy to ask the questions he was asking. He is not a wanderer but a pilgrim; he is on the road to a deeper and truer faith in Jesus.

Wherever we are, whomever we are with, we have the opportunity to remind others of God's blessing. We can remind them of their names—their *meaning* and *value,* their *origin* and *destiny,* their *place* and *purpose.* You don't have to be professionally involved in ministry to practice the art of really seeing someone. You can start by asking people to share their stories. Ask simple questions. Listen carefully. Pay attention to the Spirit—He will teach you how to bless.

What Jesus did for bread, we get to do for others. We give thanks for them, reminding them that they have come from God and that He delighted in creating them. And we rename them as carriers of the glory of God, signifying more than just what's on their birth certificate. We help them name where they have come from and where they are going, and in doing so we help them see God up close. We get to participate in the work of renaming.

What's in a Name?

Phil Knight, the founder of Nike, recounts a fantastic scene in which he began to name the various lines of athletic shoes in his newly formed company. After years of involvement with Blue

Ribbon Sports as a distributor for the Japanese shoe company Onitsuka, Knight was backed into a corner by the cutthroat tactics of Onitsuka. The only option was to form his own company and find manufacturers. When he saw the shoes that legendary coach and business partner Bill Bowerman had designed with Jeff Johnson, their first full-time employee, Knight realized he would have the honor of naming the models.

In an empty building in downtown Tokyo, without his co-creators and team, Knight had to shoulder the task alone. The first was a tennis shoe. The Wimbledon. That seemed simple enough. The next was the Forest Hill, after the setting for the first US Open. A basketball shoe became the Blazer, after Knight's home-town team in Portland, Oregon, the Portland Trail Blazers. On and on it went. In just a half hour, he named them all—tennis shoes, basketball shoes, and running shoes. Knight described the experience in his memoir:

> A feeling came over me, unlike anything I'd ever experienced. I felt spent, but proud. I felt drained, but exhilarated. I felt everything I ever hoped to feel after a day's work. I felt like an artist, a *creator*. I looked back over my shoulder, took one last look at Nissho's [their investor's] offices. Under my breath I said, "We made this."[5]

We made this. That must be what the triune God said, looking out at the world.

Yet God, the sole and sovereign creator, chose to allow Adam to participate in the work of naming. God wants humans to join His work of blessing His world. He has chosen us to carry the blessing to creation. Like Adam, we, too, are called to become God's collaborators, naming those He has made, reminding them of who they truly are.

"To name a thing," Alexander Schmemann wrote, "is to manifest the meaning and the value God gave it, to know it as coming from God and to know its place and function within the cosmos created by God."[6]

Meaning.

Value.

Origin.

Destiny.

Place.

Purpose.

This is what's in a name.

"To name a thing, in other words, is to bless God for it and in it," Schmemann concluded.[7]

You are not only blessed; you are called to carry the blessing. You have been renamed. You have been called by name. And you are to name others as God sees them. You are to help the discouraged and the lonely see themselves as chosen, holy, beloved. Find the ones worn down, breaking under their toil, and show them that the blessing is theirs. Lead them back to the God who blesses. You get to participate in this work!

There is a place where this sort of practice should occur. It's called the church. And sullied and stained as it may be, it is still the place where we remember our blessing *together*. Though all too often it has driven Hagars in despair into the wilderness, God rejoices when it functions as He created it: as a place of refuge, naming, remembrance, and blessing.

So we turn now to talk about what this looks like in church.

4

Tables

We said it was all about Jesus. We meant it. Then it was put to the test.

The public moral failure of our founding pastor shook our church in late 2006. When our new senior pastor, Brady Boyd, took over in mid-2007, the wounds among our members were still fresh. People were slow to trust another leader. Through tenderness and patience, Pastor Brady helped us begin to heal. He overhauled our church governance—the stuff you don't think really matters until it does. He gave staff members long-overdue sabbaticals and taught us how to work and rest with sustainable rhythms. He turned the focus of our church from national campaigns to local places of pain.

But we knew that even with all those positive changes, as a large church with a prominent pastor, we were prone to focusing on one individual. Yes, there was a team, and everyone was godly and humble. But still, it was a big stage, and the two most significant elements of our services highlighted individuals—the pastor or the worship leader. We needed something else to help us center the focus of our worship services on Jesus.

For us, the answer became clear: the Lord's Table.

Luke, writer of the gospel narrative that bears his name and of the book of Acts, used the phrase "the breaking of bread" as a shorthand for the Lord's Table. He included this as a regular event for the early believers (see Acts 2:42). Documents describing Christian gatherings in the decades that followed the New Testament era indicate that communion was the central practice of the early church. Many early Christians would do their best to never miss a gathering simply because they did not want to miss coming to the Lord's Table.

When Pastor Brady asked me to start a new service on Sunday nights in 2009, he encouraged me to let it be a laboratory of sorts. One of the things he specifically encouraged me to test out was weekly communion. He knew I had been pondering why Christians for so many centuries had made it the centerpiece of their worship and why contemporary American evangelicals had largely abandoned the practice. Celebrating the Lord's Table together became the cornerstone of our Sunday night services. It wasn't long before it became a weekly practice on Sunday mornings as well. A few years later, when we planted New Life Downtown as a congregation of New Life Church, we knew we would joyfully continue that practice.

Over the years of making communion our weekly practice, we've discovered something. We weren't alone in wanting to make Jesus the center of everything that was said, sung, and done on a Sunday morning. We found thousands of others who were longing for a way to be led to Jesus—simply, purely, and even liturgically. I don't mean that we thought reciting old prayers and confessions was cool or trendy. I mean there was a hunger to know that our faith is part of a long-standing, sacred tradition. It is rooted and reliable. There are revered words that others have sung and prayed—millions of others, for hundreds of years. We weren't the first to confess our sins and receive forgiveness at this Table. We weren't the only ones proclaiming the "mystery of faith"—that Christ died, was risen, and will come again. There are others. There *have been* others. We are not alone.

This may seem obvious to some, but we realized along the way that the Table was also the place where Christ alone was the focus. People in our church have always believed that there are many moments within a worship service that are particular places of encounter with the presence of God, moments where Christ's availability is acute through the Holy Spirit. Certainly, in New Life's culture, the music—worship in song—was and is one of those places. And so is the preaching. We believe that God speaks when His Word is proclaimed. But here's the thing about the music and the preaching: they rely heavily on the human element. An unskilled musician could ruin the moment; a vain preacher could steal the attention. Furthermore, both music and rhetoric are prone to manipulation.

But the Table . . . the Table is about the bread and the cup. No doubt in darker chapters of the church's history, humans have found a way to be the focal point there as well. Yet in our context the Lord's Table provided an opportunity for us as leaders to get out of the way. We are not the host of this great feast. We are like doorkeepers who welcome guests in.

Coming to the Table is a central practice for our church because of the way it is a *centering* practice. It centers our hearts and
calls our attention unmistakably to Jesus.

Where Jesus Is Available

What makes church so special that we expect to meet Jesus there?
There are many metaphors for describing the church. New Testament writers frequently referred to the church as a household or a
family. And then, of course, there's Paul's famous comparison of
the church to a body (see 1 Corinthians 12).

One of the more powerful metaphors the New Testament uses
is that of the temple. In the Old Testament the temple was the
place where the presence of God descended. It was, in Jewish
minds, "the place where heaven and earth met."[1] In fact, it was
considered the very center of the world. So when Paul began saying
that God was building the church as a new temple, the place where
God would pour out His presence, the place He would fill with all
His fullness (see Ephesians 2), his listeners may have been a bit
skeptical. Or excited.

The Jewish people in the time of Christ would have been waiting for a new temple, one that would restore God's glory in their
very midst. Yes, Herod had built one, but Herod was a complicated, compromising mess. Who is to say if he had any right to
build a holy place? Herod's temple was there, but where was the
glory of God? So when Jesus talked about Himself as the temple (as
recorded in John's gospel), the Jews around Him got nervous. Was
Jesus guilty of blasphemy? Paul, it seems, took it one step further.

Not only is Jesus the true temple, the ultimate place where heaven and earth collide, but He also formed a people who are together a new temple. God pours out His glory on this new people when they gather together.

Seriously?

Yes.

Somehow when the people of God gather in Jesus's name, God's Spirit is *there*.

This brings us to the other frequently used metaphor for the church: the body of Christ. Imagine if someone were to ask you, "Where might we find Jesus in the world today?" What would you say? The New Testament says that the fullness of God "dwells bodily" in Christ Jesus (Colossians 2:9) and that Jesus is seated at the right hand of the Father (see Romans 8:34). So the *body* of Christ, in a very real sense, is sitting next to the first person of the Trinity.

But the New Testament also says that everywhere the gathered church is, they are the body of Christ. Theologian Robert Jenson interpreted the notion of the church as Jesus's body to mean that the church is "the place where Christ is available" in the world.[2] Where the gathered church is, there is Jesus. As a matter of fact, Jesus said, "Where two or three are gathered in my name, there am I among them" (Matthew 18:20).

But there's more. Jesus said that every time we come to the Table in remembrance of Him, we are to recognize Him in the bread—the bread *is the body of Christ*.

Jesus calls bread His body, and the church is called the body of Christ.

Where is Jesus's body? In heaven, yes. But also here on earth, in the church and at the Table. It may be strange to put it that way, and that's why Robert Jenson's language again is helpful. *Christ makes Himself available to us through the church and through communion.* Now all of a sudden we see the link between the *church* and *bread.* Both are vivid pictures of the presence and availability of Christ.

When we hear the gospel writer's words that Jesus took bread, blessed it, broke it, and gave it, what if we exchange the word *bread* with the word *church*? And Jesus took the *church*—the ones the Father entrusted to His care (see John 17)—and He blessed them, broke them, and gave them for the life of the world.

REHEARSING OUR BLESSEDNESS

Church is where we become *bread.* It is where we are blessed together.

Each week, when we gather in worship as the church, we are rehearsing our blessedness in Christ. We are saying that it isn't our money or our family or our jobs or our status that makes us blessed; it is the grace of God in Jesus Christ.

When we receive communion, we come with empty hands, open and unclenched. I like this because it is a bodily expression of repentance: we have let go of the lesser things we've been holding on to. Our jobs won't save us, and our friendships won't ultimately fulfill us. So rather than grasp those things more tightly, we unclench our fists and let go.

Our open hands at communion also remind us that we've let go of the reins. The root of sin is the desire to be in charge of our own lives, to play God's role in our own story—to be the source of our own identity, to be the captain of our own destiny. But open hands are a way of saying we are not grasping for control anymore.

And the emptiness of our own hands also speaks to our own poverty. We have nothing to offer, nothing to bring to earn our keep. The Lord's Supper is not a potluck.

Then, as we come, our hands are filled with something—with bread (or a cracker or wafer meant to represent the bread). That ordinary sustenance, that daily supply, that universal staple—bread. We come to God without even the basics of survival. We have no way of caring for or providing for ourselves. We cannot nourish our own souls. We cannot be our own origins. We cannot name ourselves. Someone must do it for us. Someone must *bless* us.

Jesus does this at His Table. He blesses us by giving us Himself. "Receive my body and my blood," Jesus in essence tells us. "Let me be your portion and your cup. Where you are not enough, I am more than enough." Even if you aren't at a church where communion is a regular practice, there is something powerful here for you to see. Jesus has given Himself to be your bread and your drink. Your blessedness is not about what you bring to the table; it's what Jesus has brought to the Table—Himself. You have nothing to give. He is our all. We hear over and over that we should internalize the mantra that *we are enough.* But the Lord's Table is one place that makes us confront that lie. It frees us to say, "I'm actually not enough. And that's okay because Jesus is."

How does a church rehearse its blessedness in Christ? How do we remember that we are the body of Christ? What practice shapes us to be Christ's presence in the world? It's the Table. The Lord's Table is a central practice and a centering practice.

When the Lord's Table becomes a central and centering practice, it also becomes a core paradigm—the thing that shapes our self-understanding as the church. To put it more plainly, coming to the Lord's Table is a way of understanding the church's life and mission as the *body* of Christ in the world. One liturgical prayer asks that by power of the Holy Spirit the bread would "be for us" the body of Christ so that we "might be for the world" the body of Christ. Imagine praying that each Sunday. Just as we meet Jesus as we receive the bread, so the world meets Jesus as they receive us.

To be the family of God, you come to the Lord's Table. To be centered on Jesus, you let His body and blood be the climax of the gathering. To be the body of Christ for the world, you come to receive bread.

Who Is at the Table?

A family is formed at a table. And you don't get to choose who's at the table. We didn't get to choose the families we were born into. The disciples certainly didn't get to choose who else would be part of that first ragtag family of sorts that was formed around Jesus. Think about all the different backgrounds, passions, and walks of life that were represented at the Last Supper.

Today, when it comes to church, we often have the luxury of picking the place where we worship. I understand that finding a church can be difficult. But can it be less of a consumer decision and more of a discernment process? Even if we accept that approach, what factors should be part of our discernment? Certainly, one factor would be the people. The church, after all, is made up of men, women, and children. What kind of people do we want with us at the Table? If we are going to be formed together as a family at Jesus's Table, can we choose who will comprise that family?

Let me introduce you to Morton. When we met him, he had been homeless for a few years. Though he's loud and often late, he has become a fixture at our 11:00 a.m. Sunday service. We can always tell he's there because he bursts out in a loud, low "Hallelujah!" to announce his arrival—regardless of where we are in the service. Throughout the worship time, Morton will usually exclaim in his booming voice, "Praise the Lord!" or "Thank You, Jesus!" I have also come to expect his interjections during my sermon—"Amen!" or "Say it!"—especially when I talk about God's concern for the poor and the church's responsibility to confront injustice. There's no doubt his own life experiences make him acutely aware of things that are mostly abstract for many of our other church members.

My favorite "Mortonism" comes during the prayer of confession, which we say during each Sunday service. It's the confession from the *Anglican Book of Common Prayer:* "Merciful God, we confess that we have sinned against you in thought, and word, and deed, by what we have done, and by what we have left undone. We have not loved you with our whole heart"—and this is where Morton makes his voice heard well above the crowd—"and we have not loved our neighbors as ourselves."

The people in attendance, reciting those words, are forced to think, *Wait a minute. Morton is our neighbor. He is homeless—or at least he frequently has no place to sleep. Have we loved him as ourselves? Have we loved our neighbor as ourselves?*

Before we can fully engage in the self-reflection Morton's booming voice provoked, we are on to the next lines: "We are truly sorry, and we humbly repent. Now for the sake of your Son, Jesus Christ, have mercy on us, and forgive us, that we may delight in your will and walk in your ways, to the glory of God. Amen."

We occasionally receive questions or comments about Brother Morton. Once in a while, people don't come with a question but with a conclusion. They've decided that Morton is too distracting or inappropriate or inconsiderate in his vocal exhortations and outbursts. Some people have even said that they just can't take it anymore. The behavior is unruly and out of order, and they don't want to attend a church that puts up with it. When people arrive at this decision before inquiring about our perspective, they apparently presume we simply lack the courage to deal with this situation.

The truth is, we *know* Morton. He isn't just some *unruly* person. We know his story. One of our pastors even paid—out of his own pocket—for a membership to the local YMCA so Morton could use the showers. Several church members have given him money to get him through a pinch; others have helped him get various odd jobs. One couple in particular, Chuck and Lucy, have developed a real friendship with him that has become life changing—for all three of them.

"I had a major shift of perspective one morning," said Chuck, who befriended Morton more than a year ago. He went on to say,

Let's just say people gave Morton lots of room in the sanctuary—to the point that no one would sit in the row with him and often left space in the row behind and the row in front. So I decided to sit next to Morton.

In his inimitable way, Morton was emphasizing every third or fifth word of the worship songs, hollering out, "Faith!," "Love!," "Jesus!," or whichever word moved him. During the singing, I had a transformational moment when I realized that the day would come when Morton and I would stand before the throne worshipping together. Nothing of affluence or race or anything else on this earth would matter. We are in fact brothers, children of the same loving Father.

Chuck and Lucy's relationship with Morton began to grow into a genuine friendship. Technically, Morton "lives" near their neighborhood, sleeping under the eaves of an abandoned building near the city park. In time they began inviting him to stop by for lunch or breakfast. And Morton began to do some odd jobs around the house for them.

Their initial reaction to Morton's situation was to try to immediately solve his homelessness. But early on, Lucy was wise enough to point out that more than anything they might do for Morton, the most important thing was simply to be his friend. Once a week Chuck would bike over to the city park to visit Morton at "his" picnic bench. His constant companion was a transistor radio tuned to the Christian station twenty-four hours a day. Scripture was never far from his lips. Morton was an encouragement to

Chuck and Lucy, talking to them about patience and our call to praise the Lord in every situation.

Initially, Morton said he was content with living outside. "The raccoons and the spiders are my friends," Morton was fond of saying, poking fun at his own situation. "I'm living outside with the bums. You can call me 'Captain Caveman.'" Morton is an imposing human being, rock solid with a morning regimen of push-ups to help him stay that way. Still, nearing age sixty and now with a tumor on his spinal cord cutting off the feeling in his hands and his feet, he couldn't continue sleeping every night in a sleeping bag wrapped up in a tarp on the concrete. He finally admitted, "I need to get off the streets."

Over the next several months, Chuck went with Morton to explore the options. Morton put his name on the waiting list again for the city housing authority. "Won't hear anything from them," he said as they left the office. And he was right. They inquired at a handful of low-income housing facilities. The waiting lists were already more than a year out.

It takes a community to solve some problems. Just when it seemed there was no way to help Morton off the street, another woman in our church reached out to him with an opportunity. She had met Morton at a summer meal group. She told him about a little-known organization that exists to serve those like Morton who don't fit neatly into any category of need that would allow him to find housing. With some initial financial help from our church, Morton was approved for the transitional housing program—just a month before the surgery to remove the tumor growing on his neck. For the first time perhaps in his entire life, Morton has his own room in a warm, safe house where he can recover and get his feet on the ground.

The change in Morton is easy to see. He has hope again. He always cared about how he looks on a Sunday morning and the cleanliness of his clothing, and now because of the new housing situation, the availability of a daily shower, and laundry facilities he is able to take care of himself better.

Our perspective tends to change when we know an individual's name and story. If everyone would take time to ask about his story and listen closely, we would be less concerned with how he is interrupting our services. Maybe we would even come to see ourselves as being here for *his* sake.

If we ever become a church that has no room for Morton—or anyone like him—I no longer want to serve as its pastor. The point is not to have a church full of Mortons, just as it isn't the goal to have a church full of middle-class families. In fact, church is where the people we would have chosen and those we would *not* have chosen gather under the same roof and in the same name. Church is the kind of gathering where an outsider might look at a seemingly random assortment of people and wonder what in the world they have in common—and the only possible answer is "Jesus."

A family is formed at a table. And you don't get to choose who's at the table.

Just as the blessing came to Abraham's family, so the blessing of God through Jesus Christ comes to a new family. To be *blessed* is not to be an independent, isolated individual soaking up the blessing. To be blessed is to be part of a new family. When we are blessed in the hands of Jesus, we recover our origin and with it a new trajectory and destiny. We are given a new name and with it a new story. Finally, we are seated at a Table where we are formed into a family. This is what being blessed means in all its fullness.

One Feast, One Family

Holly and I have four children. To say life is full is like calling the Rocky Mountains a speed bump. We spend our evenings shuttling our kids between activities, carpooling friends, and making sure we haven't left a child behind at the dance studio or soccer field. With all of this hustle and bustle, dinner is often the last thing on our minds.

Don't get me wrong—I love to cook. And Holly is fantastic about finding healthy recipes and making sure our fridge and pantry are stocked with wholesome foods. But where do we find the time to chop, cut, grind, blend, bake, and boil? Our go-to midweek meal is grilled chicken and rice, since it is quick, easy, and usually a crowd pleaser. For nutritional value, we might add some green beans on the side.

So you can imagine our exasperation when we take the time to plan meals and try out a new recipe and our children say, "I don't want to eat *that*!" I want to respond, "Sorry, kids. *That* is what's for dinner." Somehow they expect that they can improvise, customize, or raid the fridge to find something different for dinner. On the evenings when we're feeling exhausted—so basically, every weekday—we may give in and switch the menu. But other times we double down and remind the dissatisfied kids that our home is not a restaurant and we are not their personal chefs. There is *one* plan for dinner, and they can take it or leave it. (Said in kinder words, of course).

Funny as all this, I think it's actually a bit like the way the kingdom of God functions. You see, there is only one table in the Father's house. To be part of the family is to share in the feast. And the reverse is also true: if you want the feast, you have to welcome the family.

The older brother in the prodigal son story found this out the hard way (see Luke 15). He complained that his father was throwing a lavish feast for his wayward younger brother and yet he, the older brother, had never been honored with such a feast. He could have enjoyed *this* one, just as he had enjoyed every other family dinner over the years. The problem was that, because of jealousy and bitterness, he could not embrace his brother. In fact, in the conversation outside the house, the older son wouldn't even name his brother as his brother. Speaking to his father, he said, "This *son of yours* . . ." (verse 30, emphasis added).

But the father wouldn't have it. In his reply, he countered by saying, "This *your brother* . . ." (verse 32, emphasis added).

We can see ourselves in this exchange. So often, we try to distance ourselves from the ones the Father keeps embracing. We'd prefer to have God to ourselves, and we'd rather enjoy a Jesus-and-me kind of Christianity. We'd rather church be the place where we gather with just a few close friends. We don't want distractions or interruptions or undesirables. We want the *feast;* we just don't want the *family.*

Here's what the older brother didn't see: he, too, had left the father's house.

The story is commonly called the parable of the prodigal son, but that is too narrowly focused. It might be more aptly called the Tale of Two Lost Brothers and One Family Table. And in the way Jesus told this parable to conclude a set of three parables, there's a buildup we must not miss. The first story is about a lost sheep. One out of a hundred sheep had gone missing, and the farmer left the ninety-nine to go in search of the one. The next story involves a lost coin. A woman had ten coins and lost one. She turned her house upside down in search of the one. In the third story a father had two sons. One asked for an early inheritance—a slap in the face to his father—and then added shame to scorn by squandering that inheritance on wicked living.

But you see, Jesus told these parables to show *escalating ratios of lostness*. Each story ups the ante, increases the probability that *His listeners* were lost. When they heard the first story, they may have thought, *One out of a hundred? Yeah, I know someone just like that. It's too bad they're not around to hear this message.* And then with the story about the coins, they may have chuckled and said, "Yeah, one out of ten—that's more like it. Lots of bad people out there." But when Jesus moved to a story about two brothers, His listeners might have felt their heart pound just a little more in their chests. "One of two? That's 50 percent! I didn't think there were *that* many rebellious, wicked people around! But, you know, things are getting worse in our world. Thank God I'm not like them!"

And when the final moment of the third parable arrived, they may finally begin to see it: *Both* brothers were lost. *Both* sons left the house.

There was no escaping it now. The people in need of saving are not *those* people. It's me: *I* need saving. *I* am lost.

This is what keeps us from welcoming others into the family. This is what prevents us from extending the blessing to people we do not like: we have forgotten that we, too, were lost. It hurts to say it. But only when we do are we able to see the stunning love of God.

You see, the father left the house to come after *both* sons. With the younger brother, in his shame and brokenness, the father held him and wept. With the older brother, in his pride and resentment, the father came to plead and persuade. The father's love wouldn't let go. God comes after us in our shame and in our pride, in our mess and in our self-righteousness. Both rebellion and religion can make us leave the Father's house. But only the love of the Father can call us home.

When you see that you, too, were lost, when you understand that all of us like sheep have gone astray—not just one out of a hundred—you understand how magnificent the mercy of God is. Oh, what love the Father has lavished on us!

There is only one table at the Father's house. And He has spread out a feast for us. Welcome the family and enjoy the feast together. This is what it means to be the church. This is what it means to be *blessed* . . . together.

BROKEN

5

Shadows and Shame

I sat there with my head down, my hands pressed against the stubble on my cheeks, unsure of how to respond. My spiritual director, a pastor who trained as a counselor and guides people toward a healthy journey with God, repeated the question. "Are you ashamed for feeling so down?"

The previous week had been unlike anything I'd ever experienced. I had returned from a week in England, part of a residency requirement for my doctorate in theology and ministry, which I had begun a year earlier. The day after arriving home, I left again on a two-day retreat with a few senior leaders from our church to dream together about the future of our ministry. I came home utterly exhausted and depleted. Then I had coffee with a couple who had been mentors to several young couples and influential within our community. It was over a mocha that they decided to tell me they were leaving the church. They said all the right things and so did I—in the moment. But it stung. I felt blindsided.

On top of all that, my wife and I were, shall we say, out of sync after my traveling. We were misreading each other, overreacting, misunderstanding, and being a little snippy. And it was all just making me sink. Low. Lower than I had ever felt before. I had thoughts that I'd never had before—voices and whispers of rejection and failure.

And there was no way in that moment, on that particular evening, to cognitively override them. I was in a deep, dark place. I kept silent, lying on the couch until late in the night, before making myself move to my bed. It took days to slowly climb out of the funk.

So when I finally went to meet with my spiritual director, a man I had been seeing once a month for a little over a year at that point, I was at least able to articulate the depths of what I had felt. But I was not yet able to make sense of it.

That's when he asked me the question: "Are you ashamed for feeling so down?"

He might have phrased it another way: "Do you think it's okay for you to be not okay?"

I knew the "right" answer.

"Sure," I said, "I don't think I have any reason to feel guilty or ashamed. I'm not sinning or anything. And I know it's okay to be sad or discouraged. But I don't know why it got me so deeply. I don't know why I sank so low."

He paused to think for a few moments, and then responded, "Glenn, it sounds like you're standing over yourself in judgment, like you're looking at the Glenn in the pit. And you're standing outside the pit, above the pit, looking down on yourself. You're shaking your head, wagging your finger, like you can't believe you're feeling this way."

The image got to me. Standing in judgment over myself. Yes, that *was* what I was doing. I wanted to disassociate myself from *that* Glenn, from whoever that was. That wasn't *me*.

That's when I realized what I was doing, that I was separating myself into different pieces, trying to disassociate myself from myself.

I suspect we all do that sometimes. There's a version of ourselves that we are pleased with and proud of . . . and there's a version we don't really like, the one we'd like to keep in the basement away from the light. Psychologists and counselors will sometimes refer to this as our "idealized self" and our "shadow self."[1]

Everybody has a shadow. Sometimes, the greater the positive projection of self, the darker the shadow lurks. You see this most clearly in public figures—celebrities, politicians, rock stars, or athletes—who convey a strong, put-together image but have doubts and fears rumbling beneath the surface.

Michael Jordan was at the peak of his career when negative press began to mount. "Sooner or later, I knew things were going to turn around," Jordan told *Sports Illustrated* journalist Jack McCallum. "Five, six, seven years at the pinnacle of success and it's going to happen. Signs are starting to show that people are tired of hearing about 'Michael Jordan's positive influence' and 'Michael Jordan's positive image.'"[2]

He was right. Maybe the young superstar had gotten famous too quickly. After all, previous basketball stars, such as Julius Erving, had become legends over the course of their careers. Here was Jordan, not even thirty years old and a global superstar. And he had a decade or so of dominance ostensibly ahead of him.

But Jordan was not naive about human psychology. Not only was he aware of his own dark side, but he also knew that even an adoring public had to discover that darkness in order to understand that he was human. "What I was trying to do was project everything positive, and maybe that was wrong," he said. "Maybe people wanted to see some negative with the positives, so that they'd have more of a sense of you as a human being. I accept that. . . . The negative stuff, the backlash, is coming down on me, and heck, I'm at the peak of my career."[3]

The brighter the lights, the larger the shadow looms.

Nearly every pastor can relate to the feeling Jordan was describing—of being in the spotlight, of feeling the need to project the best parts of ourselves. This is done, of course, in an effort to be an icon of Christ. The calling, after all, is to invite others to follow you as you follow Christ. Any part of yourself that does not resemble Christ is buried in the basement. Why wouldn't the disintegration of self be the obvious occupational hazard of being in vocational ministry?

Back to my meeting with my spiritual director. He continued with more insight.

"Jesus is with *that* Glenn, down in the pit. Jesus loves *that* Glenn. And Jesus loves the Glenn who is standing outside and above the pit too. He holds both together. He blesses both."

I started to tear up.

There is a light that shines in the darkness. There is a God in whom there are no shadows. There is One for whom even darkness is not dark.

There is Jesus descending into the pit, placing His hand of blessing on the shadow we'd like to shake, and extending His other hand to the proud self we think we made. He blesses both and pulls them together.

God does not see a person's idealized self and shadow self. He does not see two Glenns or two yous.

You might be standing over yourself in judgment because you don't quite feel good enough—as a friend, as a mom or a dad, as a wife or a husband, as a daughter or a son. Maybe you've made some mistakes. Maybe you've hit your limit and started to crack. Maybe those cracks have made you aware of how broken you really are. But you don't like that you; you would rather paper over the breaks and soldier on.

And yet.

In our *brokenness,* we are *beloved.* In our frailty, God remains faithful.

The truth is, there is only one self: one you, one me. And I am, and you are, deeply loved.

Believing that and receiving that is how brokenness does not become a fracture. Instead, our brokenness can let the grace of God come rushing in.

FRAILTY AND FAILURE

Jesus took bread, blessed it, and broke it.

I imagine the bread to be like roti, that delicious flatbread I grew up eating in Malaysia. It was soft, ready to dip in a bowl of lentil curry. But when broken, it was as if its pores opened up. The man at the shop would scoop it from the flat hot surface on which it had been cooking, and he would smash it from end to end, making flakes fall to the sides. It became fluffy and airy. From there, the one eating could easily break off a piece, revealing all the little chambers for the curry to rush into.

I know the bread Jesus broke at the Last Supper was not quite like that. And yet there is something about broken bread that makes it ready to absorb olive oil, curry, or sauce of any kind. It's the very act of breaking bread that makes it ready to soak up something.

Could that be what happens to us? Could it be that God's grace comes rushing into the very brokenness of our lives? Maybe brokenness has a way of opening us up to the Lord. The more aware we become of our frailty, the more we are able to embrace the grace of God. "My strength is made perfect in weakness," the Lord told the apostle Paul (2 Corinthians 12:9, NKJV). Or as Leonard Cohen sang, "There is a crack, a crack in everything. That's how the light gets in."[4]

To be broken is to be opened up to grace.

But *brokenness* can be a tricky word. We use it sometimes to refer to our frailty, to our humanness, to our earthy state. But we also use it as a metaphor for our sin, our shortcomings, our failure. In a way, the word *brokenness* is a little like the New Testament's word *flesh.* Sometimes *flesh* is used to refer to our physicality and with it our mortality. Other times *flesh* means our carnality—the part of us under the power of sin, lived out in opposition to God and His rule. The meanings overlap: one is true because of the other.

Our flesh is mortal because it is carnal. Or to put it in Paul's terms in Romans, *death* entered the world through *sin* (see Romans 5:12).

So there is an overlap between our frailty and our failure; human beings are frail because of the original failure of the first humans. Yet there are differences. There is no need to feel shame for being frail or fragile or weak, for wrestling with fear or doubt or hurt. These are all reminders that we are earthen vessels, jars of clay. It's no sin to be mortal. It's not your fault that you're finite.

But what about the other kind of brokenness? What about when we fail? Is there a kind of shame that springs from something deeper, not from *frailty* but from *failure*?

GUILT AND SHAME

We may argue about evidence for the existence of God, for the resurrection of Christ, for the virgin birth, and more. But most of us do not struggle to find evidence of what the Bible calls sin. We *know* we've missed the mark, fallen short, and not measured up. Deep in our bones, we know guilt and the shame that comes with it.

We sometimes hear that such feelings are merely the result of negative social conditioning. To say it plainly, one common modern-day view is that humans have been brainwashed by religion into feeling guilty and ashamed about things that shouldn't make them feel that way. Some people go even further by saying that guilt and shame are artificial constructs developed by those in power in order to oppress others—that guilt and shame are tools used by the powerful to manipulate others.

No doubt religion *has* been misused in these ways. The historical examples are widespread. While we acknowledge the existence of unnecessary shame and manipulative guilt, we seem to know deep down inside that's not where *all* guilt and shame come from. Indeed, the experience of guilt and the consequences of wrongdoing are woven throughout the history of human civilizations.

There are ruins in modern-day Turkey that are dated among the oldest monuments in the world. Archaeologists believe these structures are about twelve thousand years old, far older than anything previously discovered. The site provides the first indication of a community trying to settle down, the beginning attempts to live in a civilization rather than as a wandering group of hunters and scavengers. Some archaeologists say that this discovery, made a couple of decades ago, will revolutionize how we think about the origins of civilization. But I wonder if it's also going to change the way we think about religion.

You know why? Because at the heart of this primal collection of structures is a *temple*.

The Göbekli Tepe is the oldest known temple in the world, located in the oldest collection of buildings in the world, belonging to the earliest civilization known to archaeologists. Think of it: the first group of humans to settle down in a place built a temple. The site was likely a gathering point, and the mound of tens of thousands of buried animal bones seem to indicate that it was also a site of great feasting.

But there's more. Mini versions of the Göbekli Tepe were built in other settlements up to 125 miles away, leading to speculation that the Göbekli Tepe was a "cathedral and the others local churches." One theory is that "hunter-gatherers might have traveled long distances to meet, worship and help build new monumental structures, sponsoring feasts to display their wealth."[5]

Isn't it interesting that one of the oldest archaeological discoveries of humans building something together includes a site of worship?

We don't know what sort of religion was practiced or what kind of worship was conducted. But from this early indication that humans seemed instinctively compelled to worship a divine being, we can follow the story of ancient religions and note the impulse to offer sacrifices, often in the attempt to appease the gods.

To put it plainly, humans have seemed unable to escape the notion that there is a god or several gods and that the god or gods are distant at best and angry at worst. *The gods are angry, and humans are guilty.*

I grew up in a country with various religions, many of them reaching back thousands of years. Buddhism, Hinduism, and Islam are among the great religions of the world found in my homeland. Granted, none of these are derivatives of or even vaguely comparable with religions from biblical times. But they share the same premise: the gods are distant, possibly even angry, and it's probably our fault.

None of this proves anything about the origin of sin or the reason we experience guilt and shame. But it ought to make us more cautious of dismissing guilt and shame as made-up responses used to oppress the masses. Sin, guilt, and shame seem to be nearly as old as civilization.

What Shame Is Trying to Say

Let me pause to reiterate that some shame *should* be cast off. There is a kind of shame that is not connected with any wrongdoing; in fact, it's often a shame that comes from being the victim. That kind of shame can and should be met with an affirmation of self, with a reminder of our dignity and worth, with a belief in our blessedness in Christ.

But part of the trouble is we've dumped all shame into the same pot and thrown the whole thing out as a toxic brew.

Ours is a skeptical age. We've seen too much, been sold too much, been fooled too many times, been hurt and disappointed and let down. We've been beaten down and held there by a lie. We're tired of it. We don't want to feel bad anymore. We won't let anyone tell us we're wrong. In fact, we've decided that shame is not something we should ever feel, even when it's attached to guilt. After all, guilt is all relative anyway. What's wrong to you may not be wrong to me. So if my truth is different than your truth, then I won't let your truth shame me.

We have no use for shame and little patience for guilt.

But what if there is a kind of healthy shame, one that actually serves a purpose? What if it is there to tell us something, like the indicators on the dashboards of our cars, forcing us to consult the manual just to figure out what it means?

Sociologist Randall Collins has spent years studying "interaction ritual chains," the ways groups act to form solidarity. He wrote, some decades ago, that shame is the result of a breakdown of solidarity. When you let the group down, when you fail to keep up your end of the bargain, when you fall short on what others were counting on you for, when you drop the ball and erode trust . . . then you feel shame.

This is the kind of shame that is connected to wrongdoing. It is a shame that comes from guilt. This is why trying to retain the concept of guilt while seeking to eliminate the feeling of shame simply won't work. No matter how good you get at self-talk, no matter how many mantras you memorize, if you break solidarity with the group—your society, your community, your friends, your neighbors—you feel it. Not all shame is the result of guilt, but all guilt results in shame.

Collins says that some tribes create a counter-ritual to restore the offender into the group. It involves the offender facing the anger of the offended and seeing the impact of his or her wrongdoing. In this way, the violator is "ritually punished" and then allowed to be reintegrated into the group.[6]

Some version of this occurs in our Western justice systems. The accused may face his accusers in court, offer a defense or a plea of guilt, and then accept his punishment. What is missing, of course, is the chance to reintegrate into the group. This stops short of the type of restorative justice we long for. Guilt leads to shame, and shame can only be broken when the wrongdoer faces the anger of the wronged and is punished in order to be reintegrated into the group.

Makes sense. We can see this at work in our own group of friends.

But what if the person we have wronged is *God*? Who can face down the anger of God?

And live?

We need something stronger than self-talk and self-esteem. We need someone to stand on our behalf. We need a *priest*.

Where have you felt shame that is connected to guilt or wrongdoing? Have you experienced the sense that you have not simply let a friend down but actually offended God? What if the private sins that you think don't really affect another person are actually insults to God? When you know you've acted in a way that cuts against the grain of the universe, when you know you've participated in the degradation of another human being, when you feel like you've taken poison into your own soul, that's when you know this isn't just social conditioning. This is more than negative self-talk. This is not unhealthy shame. This is *guilt* and the rightly accompanying *shame*.

Who can take it away? Will this be a brokenness that ends in ruin? Can you be blessed even as you are broken? Does the brokenness of sin eliminate the possibility of coming under the blessing?

The Blessing That Heals Our Brokenness

The earliest archives of world religion show that priests provided two main things: access to gods and the acquisition of their blessing on many different endeavors. A priest would petition the gods for favors, rain, victory in battle, and more. A priest had special access because of his own restricted way of living.

Priesthood in Israelite religion, as recorded in the Old Testament, had some similarities. But it also had four huge distinctions:

First, the God of Israel was the only God you needed to talk to. There was no need to run around completing a long to-do list of errands at various temples for various blessings for various needs. One God was sovereign over all. If you came to Him, He was enough.

Second, the God of Israel was not fundamentally an angry god. He gets angry, but He *is* love. When Moses asked for a glimpse of God, "the LORD passed before him and proclaimed, 'The LORD, the LORD, a God merciful and gracious, slow to anger, and abounding in steadfast love and faithfulness'" (Exodus 34:6). This is who the God of Israel *is:* loving, compassionate, and gracious. He doesn't view humans as a nuisance to be tolerated for the tasks they take off His plate; He isn't looking for opportunities to strike them down. He is *slow to anger* but *abounding* in steadfast love.

Third, because the God of Israel is compassionate and gracious, He forbade human sacrifice. While not every religion in the ancient Middle East required human sacrifice, many did, and we are hard pressed to find places where it is forbidden. But the Old Testament provides a long and famous story about the God of Israel asking for a display of devotion in the only language for devotion that a pagan would understand—child sacrifice—and then revealing Himself as the God who provides the sacrifice He requires. This is where God becomes the *God of Abraham,* by showing Himself as the God who *provides.*

Fourth—and this is where it gets really good—the God of Israel provided a sacrifice specifically for the removal of guilt.[7] The most dramatic way sin was dealt with in Israel's worship came on the day of the year known as the Day of Atonement. On that day the high priest would first offer sacrifices to cleanse himself. Then he would select two goats. After laying hands on one goat and imparting to it all the sins of the nation, the priest would lead that goat out into the wilderness. Do you catch the meaning of the act? The goat took the *blame* and was led away—a picture, an enacted parable, of God removing all guilt from His people. The second goat was sacrificed and its blood was sprinkled on the altar inside the holy of holies. This goat took the *punishment*—a picture of God allowing the people to be spared judgment.

These elaborate and symbolic acts were found only in the Israelite religion. Their God was the only god who made a way to deal with sin, guilt, and shame.

God doesn't just want to give us the surface blessings of material increase and victories in life. He wants to give us the *core blessing:* the blessing that erases our guilt and shame, the blessing that deals with our sin. You get the feeling that Israel understood this. One of the well-loved songs exclaims, "Blessed is the one whose transgression is forgiven, whose sin is covered" (Psalm 32:1).

You see, even in the *brokenness* of our own sin, we can find a *blessing* that removes guilt. When we place our sin-broken lives in the hands of Jesus, *that* brokenness becomes the brokenness of repentance. And then the blessing of forgiveness flows into us.

All the stuff about goats, priests, temples, and sacrifices was just a foreshadowing of what was to come.

There is one Priest who was also the sacrifice and, in fact, also the temple.

He was so great that He summed up in Himself all the three main components of old Israelite religion. And in doing so, He brought it to its fulfillment, to its culmination, and to its closure.

His name is Jesus. Jesus, the great high priest. Jesus, the perfect sacrifice. Jesus, the true temple.

The writer of the letter to the Hebrews was so excited about the way these symbols and elements of Israelite worship came to their fulfillment in Jesus that he could hardly contain himself. Like a good preacher, he began by asking rhetorical questions, hoping for an "Amen":

> If the blood of goats and bulls and the ashes of a young
> cow, sprinkling those who are defiled, sanctify for the
> purification of the flesh, how much more will the blood
> of Christ, who through the eternal Spirit offered himself
> without blemish to God, cleanse our consciences from
> dead works so that we can serve the living God? (Hebrews
> 9:13–14, CSB)

There was an old blessing, a prayer, that the high priest in Israel would say over the people of God: "The LORD bless you and keep you; the LORD make his face to shine upon you and be gracious to you; the LORD lift up his countenance upon you and give you peace" (Numbers 6:24–26). Because of Jesus, every word of that blessing is now true for all who belong to Him. It is no longer a *petition* but a *proclamation*. Hear it over you: "The Lord blesses you and keeps you; the Lord is smiling at you; the Lord is turned toward you and gives you peace."

Jesus is the high priest who made the high priest's prayer come true.

Jesus is how God has brought you *peace*.

THE BLESSED BROKENNESS

Peace in the Bible is stronger than calm feelings; it runs deeper than the absence of turmoil. "Peace" is our weak way of translating the Hebrew *shalom*, that great word for the wholeness of the world, the completion of creation, the sense that things have come back together and been made alive.

The end of brokenness is shalom. It is brokenness that opens us up to grace, and grace that puts us together. The goal, as my spiritual director reminded me, is not the elimination of our shadow or of our brokenness. The real goal is integration—to be able to hold together every part of who we are and to see it in a new light. The goal is to let the grace of God redeem and restore and repair.

We were talking about these ideas one day with friends in our home after a meal, and one of them shared a story about an old Japanese art of mending broken pottery. *Kintsugi* means "golden joinery."[8] It's the art of joining broken pieces of pottery with a liquid resin that resembles gold. The result is a bowl or vase that is more beautiful, more aesthetically complex, and more valuable than the original piece.

Isn't that amazing? The new piece with golden seams became so popular among Japanese art collectors in the fifteenth century that some were even accused of purposely breaking pottery in order to repair it with gold.[9]

That sounds like grace. Grace takes what is broken and puts it back together in such a way that it is more beautiful and more valuable than it was before.

Where is the brokenness in your life? Is it from frailty or is it from failure? Is it your shadow or is it your sin? Do not let shame turn brokenness into fracture. Disintegration is the path to death. It may feel better to hide it or bury it or tuck it away. But don't.

Let your brokenness open you up.

To the light. To love. To the grace of God.

And when grace comes rushing in, it does not leave us broken in our sin. It heals and restores and cleanses and forgives. It makes us new in a way that is more beautiful than we could have imagined.

Grace is the gold that holds the broken pieces together.

6

Suffering and Pain

We hadn't really seen each other in years. We lost touch shortly after their wedding, apart from the occasional chance meeting around town. So when Ron and Nancy showed up in the children's ministry check-in line at church one Sunday morning, my wife was elated. Holly came and found me in the auditorium to tell me they were there.

After cheerful hugs and a brief before-service chat, I went to get ready for the start of the service. I was preaching that day on Psalm 23, on the longing in us to have someone watch over us, and how Jesus has come to fulfill that role. I could see Ron smiling during the sermon, nodding his head, leaning forward eagerly at various points. When the service was over, I went over to Ron to say again how good it was to see him. He had tears in his eyes.

"You have no idea how that spoke to me today, Glenn," he said. "Someday I'll share my story with you of the ups and downs of the past few years. It's been a journey, man."

Well, that was all I needed. We emailed the next day to set up a time for lunch. A week later at a local café, Ron filled me in on all that had taken place over the past decade. He kept using a phrase that stood out to me.

"I was a broken man."

He used it to mark two major low points in his journey. The first came after a back injury that ended his career as a firefighter. It was a devastating blow. He had been on the path to a promotion when the accident happened. His crew had been like a brotherhood, the community he had longed for. Yet after his forced retirement, they were nowhere to be found. He felt abandoned and forgotten. And in excruciating daily pain.

That's when depression set in. Alone with painkillers and no sense of purpose, Ron felt himself spiraling lower and lower. Then came the drinking. It was as if he willingly rolled the dice on his survival by draining a half dozen bottles of beer after taking pain meds. Some nights, he knew his dance with death was getting dangerously close to the precipice, and as he got into bed, he'd lean over to tell his wife goodbye in case he choked on vomit in his sleep.

Then one day, he found himself locked in the bathroom staring at a gun in his own hands, ready to end it all, convincing himself his death would make it possible for his wife and newborn child to have a better life. He couldn't take it—not the pain, not the loneliness, not the sense of emptiness, not the loss of purpose. But in that moment, he remembered God—the God he used to turn to, pray to, and believe in. He thought of his child growing up without him. And he put the gun down. He began to find help. He threw away the painkillers, stopped drinking, and began to pray again.

It was not an easy road back. But eventually Ron entered a different career, this time in real estate. Part of a highly successful brokerage that doesn't usually hire rookies, he started to rise. Through hard work, determination, and the support of his wife, he even began winning awards and setting sales records. Then came the women and late-night rendezvous over drinks that he could justify as networking. It was once again a dance with death, but this time it felt good.

"It felt so nice to my ego, to my pride," he told me. "I loved the attention."

He did not break his marriage vows, though he came close. Like Icarus, he realized how easy it was for him to fly closer and closer to the sun. And he knew what fall would await his choices.

This was the second time he used the phrase "I was a broken man."

Ron made the connection between the two experiences plain for me. "I've been in the depths, and I've been at the heights," he said. "I've been broken in both places. I almost lost it all both times."

THIRSTY

The week I meet Ron for lunch, I was preparing a sermon on Psalm 42. It struck me how much his story resembled that of the psalmist.

> I am deeply depressed;
> therefore I remember you from the land of Jordan

and the peaks of Hermon, from Mount Mizar.
Deep calls to deep in the roar of your waterfalls;
all your breakers and your billows have swept over me.
(Psalm 42:6–7, CSB)

From the peaks of mountains to the depths of the waters, he remembered God. Out of a deep depression, he remembered God.[1]

Actually, he first remembered the *people of God*—the community he used to gather with, be on pilgrimage with, worship with.

I remember this as I pour out my heart:
how I walked with many,
leading the festive procession to the house of God,
with joyful and thankful shouts. (verse 4, CSB)

When we find ourselves in broken places, this is not the cue to launch a self-help project. No amount of trying to pull ourselves up by our own bootstraps is going to work. We need others: counselors, psychologists, psychiatrists, friends, pastors, priests, and neighbors. It takes walking with many.

But the company we keep is only as good as the place they are heading. Friends can journey with you to destruction. Drinking buddies can lead you to quench your thirst with things that will never satisfy.

And that's the thing about broken places: they make us thirsty. The question is, will we thirst *for God*? Will we direct our longings toward God Himself?

The company the psalmist longs for are the people who are on their way to God, the ones who will help him again direct his thirst toward God.

He opens his prayer by naming his thirst and aiming his thirst toward God, the living God.

> As a deer longs for flowing streams,
> so I long for you, God.
> I thirst for God, the living God.
> When can I come and appear before God? (verses 1–2, csb)

There is a brokenness that can come from our frailty, and a brokenness that can come from sin; we explored both in the previous chapter. But there is a third kind of brokenness, a brokenness no one chooses. It's the kind that comes from the brokenness of the world itself. It isn't just our *frailty* or our *failure;* it's the *fallenness* of the world. It isn't simply our shadow or our sin; it's a sense that something is deeply wrong with the universe. And it breaks us.

Do you know this pain? Have you felt the crushing weight of unexpected illness, chronic pain, deep loneliness, or the loss of a job or a dream or a friend or a spouse?

Life has a way of leaving us parched. What will we do with our thirst?

There is a refrain the psalmist keeps coming back to, over and over again. Three times in Psalm 42 and Psalm 43—which may have been one song originally—this chorus appears every five verses or so. As a songwriter, I often begin writing a song by writing a chorus. The chorus is like the North Star of a song; it tells what the song is about and reminds me where all the verses are going. And so it is with the refrain in Psalms 42 and 43:

> Why, my soul, are you so dejected?
> Why are you in such turmoil?
> Put your hope in God, for I will still praise him,
> my Savior and my God. (42:5, 11; 43:5, CSB)

In the midst of suffering and pain and dryness and brokenness, there is hope yet to be found. And it is found in God. Why?

> The LORD will send his faithful love by day;
> his song will be with me in the night—
> a prayer to the God of my life. (42:8, CSB)

The Lord will send—"command," one translation says—His faithful love. We don't have the right English words for this Hebrew word *hesed*. It is used to speak of God's covenantal love, God's unfailing love, God's steadfast love. It is God's love that meets us at the mountaintops and the ocean depths. God's love holds us when the world all around us is breaking. Over and over again throughout the psalms, the songs and prayers return to this love.

Even in our brokenness, we are *loved*. We experience a love that will not let go, that will not leave us, that will not forget or forsake us. Even in brokenness, we are beloved.

And so we still praise Him. After all, it is His song that is with us in the night.

HOLY WOUNDS

The night, nevertheless, is dark. We forget things in the dark. It is easy to lose our way.

I have had the holy privilege of walking with people through their nights, but never more so than with my Ethiopian friend, Bemnetayehu.

I had just returned from a church mission trip to Swaziland when my phone rang. My wife and kids were out of town, and I had gathered the team at our house for a cookout, a chance to look at pictures and mark the memories of the trip.

I didn't want to answer my phone. So I didn't.

But he called back. I let it ring.

Then he texted saying he needed to talk to me. I called back and knew something was terribly wrong from the sound of his voice.

"She's been in an accident. She's not going to make it, bro."

I got the details about the hospital and drove straight there. I sat in a waiting room until I finally decided to go and speak with someone at the desk. They told me to go in. I found Bemnetayehu in a private room, meant for chaplains and loved ones of patients to talk.

I don't remember his first words to me, but I remember embracing him. And then we sat in silence, with an occasional phrase that spilled out from his lips—some question or lament, some way of coming to terms with the strange and sudden news that his wife was now dead.

After that tragic night, Bemnetayehu and I began meeting once a week, just to talk, pray, and cry. After two years of meeting weekly, we scaled back to meeting once a month. Then we met even less frequently. But over the course of more than three years of walking with him, sitting with him, crying with him, talking with him, I learned so much.

Bemnetayehu taught me about grief. He taught me what not to say to someone whose world has come apart. He taught me about hope. And lament. And unanswerable questions.

Often he would come with a list of things to talk about. I let him set the agenda. Sometimes it was about a verse from Scripture. Other times it was about whether I thought he should ever remarry. Sometimes he would tell me what he had been reading and which books were helpful in grief and which most certainly were not.

It's not difficult to show your scars; it's much harder to reveal your wounds. To let others into your pain in real time, to allow them to see that tender place of brokenness, to allow them to hear your questions, your off-the-cuff reflections, your in-the-moment vows—that is hard to do.

But he let me in. To those moments. To those places. To those holy wounds.

Nobody chooses to be broken this way. No one wants that as part of her story. But we break because the world is broken. Creation groans, as Paul wrote (see Romans 8:22). Aching, longing, waiting for redemption. Imagine it: the whole world, the cosmos, all of creation once blessed by God, feels itself under chains. The world God called good is subject to slavery. It has become less than itself, unable to flourish. It has lost its shalom. It is no longer whole, and so it groans.

And when the fracturing of the world touches us, when the shifting plates of the ground beneath us split apart our soul within, the brokenness is no longer *out there*. It's *in here*. It's real.

It isn't just creation that groans. It's we who groan. The gasping, grasping, out-of-breath aching; the sad, sighing, sorrowful crying—when will it end? How long, O Lord? Will You forget us forever?

BROKEN IN A BROKEN WORLD WITH BROKEN PEOPLE

But God has not forgotten us. He has not forgotten the world He made and blessed. That which God blesses is never abandoned. Brokenness is not abandonment.

The Israelites never believed in a distant God. Unlike the cultures around them, they always knew their covenant God was attentive to them and responsive to them. Their relationship was dynamic, not static. It was not a one-way thing. What He said and did moved them, and what they said and did moved *Him*.

So it should not have been surprising when God came even nearer. He came nearer than anyone dared hope. The second Person of the Trinity became flesh and was born of a virgin.

In a messy, smelly place surrounded by animals, Jesus came. As a helpless, crying baby, Jesus came.

Messy. Helpless. Crying. These are not the usual words we use to describe Jesus. Even our Christmas carols try to sanitize the scene: sweet little Jesus, "no crying He makes." Those words may make a better song, but they rob us of the richness of what God did. God came into *our* mess, into *this* blessed and broken world.

And He cried. Like a baby.

Jesus is God groaning with us.

So when it came time to preach at the funeral for Bemneta-yehu's wife, there was only one text that my heart kept being drawn to. It was the story of Jesus weeping at Lazarus's death. In these moments, in these places of brokenness and pain, we need the God who groans with us.

I knew the story in John 11 contained the verse "Jesus wept," but I had not realized the other moments in the story when Jesus *groaned,* right before and shortly after He wept (see John 11:33, 38, NKJV). In fact, the word in these verses suggests a grunt, an inarticulate moaning or sighing, like the sound an animal might make. And even more striking is what caused Jesus to groan. It was the sight of people grieving. Think of it: when God sees us groaning under the weight of the brokenness of this world, He Himself enters the groaning of creation and groans with us.

Before this moment of groaning and weeping in John 11, Jesus encountered the ones He loved, the ones who had lost their brother. Martha came to Jesus first. She said something that comes very near to an accusation: "Lord, if you had been here, my brother would not have died" (verse 21). Jesus presented Himself as her answer: "I am the resurrection and the life" (verse 25).

But when Mary came, she crumpled at His feet in tears, echoing her sister's sentiment. And Jesus Himself began to weep.

Oh, Mary. I weep with you.

Grief is like that: sometimes all we have are questions, and sometimes all we have are tears. For both—our questions and our tears—Christ Himself is the answer. Christ, the resurrection and the life, weeps with us.

I wonder if Jesus may have been thinking of his friends Mary and Martha when He later sat at a table with friends, took bread, and said, "This is my body which is broken for you" (1 Corinthians 11:24, NKJV). His very life was an offering, for the sinner and the sufferer. As that bread was broken, He knew it would sop up all our weeping, tears, and groans and would one day make all things whole again.

Maybe if Mary and Martha had been there at the Passover table, they would have understood more deeply Jesus's words, "I am the resurrection and the life." They would've glimpsed how Jesus would be broken for all of us. They may have had a foretaste of how Jesus not only walked in our broken world but also shouldered all our brokenness. Even in the brokenness of death, we are not alone. The psalmist prayed with hope, saying that God is "near to the brokenhearted" (Psalm 34:18). Jesus took that prayer and embodied it. In Jesus, God came near to all of us. No, more than that: in Jesus, God became the broken.

"This is my body which is broken for you."

REDEMPTION OVER PREVENTION

The question that both Martha and Mary asked—in fact, the question that those around them asked—is the very question that haunts us in our suffering. It's the question that arises every time pain is disconnected from justice, when suffering is the result not of guilt but of the brokenness of the world.

Couldn't you have prevented this, God?

When a person suffers needlessly, when pain seems random, or worse, unjust, the appeal to the God of mercy and justice rings throughout Scripture. *How long, O Lord? Why do the righteous suffer?*

Or in the case of Lazarus, "See how much [Jesus] loved him!" This is set right next to "He healed the eyes of the man born blind. Couldn't he have kept Lazarus from dying?" Jesus *loved* his dear friend, so why did he die?

It's not as though Lazarus was an enemy of God or a wicked person. This must have caused Mary and Martha to wonder: *Is there no justice in the world? Is there no compassion from God?* Or as, centuries later, Saint Teresa of Avila quipped after being thrown from her horse into a river on a visit to one of her monasteries, "Dear Lord, if this is how You treat Your friends, no wonder You have so few."[2]

What we often hope for from God is *prevention*. In the face of the brokenness of the world, we want to be spared. We do not want to be bent or bruised by the brokenness of a groaning world. Yet for reasons beyond our grasp, God chooses not to major in prevention. It's not that He never prevents; He often does. And frankly, it's difficult for us to know all that He has prevented. In fact, Jesus even taught us to pray that we might be spared the great day of trouble, trial, and testing.

Yet God opts for something He must know is stronger than prevention, something we call *redemption*.

You see it in this Lazarus story. While we often call what Lazarus experienced "resurrection," this is not quite right. Lazarus was raised only to die again, so this is more accurately described as "resuscitation." He was not raised in the same way that Jesus would be raised: with a perfected and glorified body that is incorruptible. Don't get me wrong—I'm sure Lazarus was thrilled to experience it! But *resurrection* is what awaits all who are in Christ. The resuscitation that Lazarus experienced was a sign of the resurrection to come. It is a clue suggesting what God will do about the brokenness of the world.

Resurrection doesn't tiptoe around death. It breaks death's power completely. Resurrection is the reversal and undoing of death. That's the power of redemption. Just as resurrection is stronger than death, so redemption is more powerful than prevention.

Imagine an artist who works a public piece, like a mural on a wall or a building. Imagine her choosing to leave her work out in the open, no ropes or cones restricting access. It is one kind of strength for an artist to prevent her work from being vandalized; it is another to say, "Whatever you scribble on this piece, I will find a way to make it even more beautiful than it was before."

Now imagine a chess player, unafraid of his opponent's strategy. It is a certain kind of genius for a chess player to block the moves his opponent wishes to make; it's a different order of brilliance altogether to say, "Whatever your move, I will still put you in checkmate."

It is one kind of power to say, "You shall not harm me!" It is a wholly other kind of power to say, "Do your worst; I will prevail."

On the cross, Jesus absorbed the full weight of evil and the judgment of God against it. Jesus became the sin that leads to death, and He became the curse that infects God's world. He drained the venom from the serpent and drank the poison to the last. He died the death that is at once sin's wage and God's verdict.

And on the third day, the Father raised Him up from the dead. The beloved Son of God experienced a love that is stronger than death. Now because of His resurrection, one day death will be swallowed up in victory. Only God can do this. Only God can take *brokenness* and bring *blessedness* from it. Only God can make blessedness *come through* brokenness.

This is why Saint Augustine wrote, "God judged it better to bring good out of evil than not to permit any evil to exist."[3]

A later Easter hymn summing up the fall of humankind in the Garden of Eden drew on Augustine's words: *"O felix culpa quae talem et tantum meruit habere redemptorem."*[4] In English: "O happy fault that merited such and so great a redeemer."

Felix culpa. Happy fault. Or blessed fall.

How can the Fall be *blessed*? Because God can bring blessedness from brokenness.

Whether the brokenness is from our frailty, our failure, or the fallenness of the world, we are still God's image bearers and this is still God's world—the world that He created, the world that He blessed. The sin and suffering God did not prevent are not beyond His capability to redeem. What God *blesses,* He will *redeem.* He has the power to make His blessing come to pass, over and against the infection of evil. God the creator blesses; God the redeemer carries the blessing to its completion, even through the brokenness that comes.

God's redemption makes even the broken become blessed. God did this by becoming the broken. In Jesus, the blessed God became the broken human so that broken humans might become God blessed.

7

Confession and Community

On any given Saturday morning, our youngest child used to awaken Holly and me at dawn, holding her stomach in agony and pleading for breakfast. You might think she had been living in a Dickensian orphanage, deprived of bread and water. She may have woken up only ten minutes earlier, but it was at that precise moment that she needed food. Or else she would starve.

Over time, she and her older brother gave up on waiting for us to rouse from our slumber. And so it was that on one such morning, when she was five and he was eight, while my wife and I attempted to sleep in to that luxurious hour of 7:00 a.m., we heard a crash from the kitchen. As I stumbled down the stairs, I found these famished early birds with brooms in their hands, oatmeal on the floor, and shattered white dishware scattered around them.

"What happened?" I asked, probably in a weary, impatient tone.

"We were making oatmeal," one of them responded, sounding defensive.

The other child provided backup. "Yeah, Dad, we were *starving,* so we decided to make our own oatmeal."

They had successfully gotten a bowl down from the cupboard, poured the oatmeal into the bowl, filled the bowl up with water, and placed the bowl in the microwave—all with minimal spillage. But the trick came with removing the hot bowl from the microwave. It was hotter than anticipated and their reflexes were instinctive and instant. *Crash!* But if they had made it that far without asking for help, then, by golly, they weren't going to give up now. And so it came to be that in one swift moment, they had squandered oatmeal, smashed a glass bowl, and sacrificed a perfectly good broom.

Surveying the mess, I asked, "Why didn't you ask me for help to clean it up?"

"Dad, we didn't want you to know about it," the five-year-old declared. "We were just going to clean it up on our own."

My heart melted. I had to admire their determination.

But it was also one of those parenting moments when I realized this was a glimpse into what I do with my Father in heaven. *I* am the kid who gets tired of waiting for my daily bread, decides to take matters into my own hands, ends up making a big mess of things, and tries to clean up the mess on my own, usually only making it worse. It's hard enough to ask for help. But it's even harder when asking for help requires admitting that we're in a mess of our own making.

Our brokenness requires that we ask for help, that we reach beyond ourselves for what we cannot find within ourselves. And very often, that request for help will require an accompanying admission of guilt.

"I'm sorry. Please help me."

Talk about pulling down our fences and breaking down our walls. We want to be able to handle it, fix it, and deal with it on our own. This is *my* life, *my* story, *my* mess, we tell ourselves. If I'm broken, then it's *my* brokenness. It's not anyone else's business.

But at some point, we're going to have to let someone else in.

COMMUNAL CONFESSION

King David certainly did not want to.

David had essentially arranged for the murder of his friend Uriah to cover up sleeping with Uriah's wife and getting her pregnant. He had tried other more discreet ways of covering his tracks, but when they all failed, arranging for Uriah to die in battle was David's final grasp at covering his own sin.

That's a lot to ignore. Yet David was so numb to his own sin that it took a prophet's confrontation for him to notice it. The prophet Nathan told King David a dramatic story about two men in a city, one rich and the other poor, one with plenty of sheep and the other with only one ewe lamb. When a traveler came to visit the rich man, the man did not want to use any of his own flock to feed the traveler, so he took the poor man's only lamb, the lamb that the poor man had fed and nurtured. David was outraged at the story. Invoking God's name, King David declared that the rich man ought to restore sevenfold to the poor man. And then Nathan the prophet delivered his mic-drop line: "You are the man!" (2 Samuel 12:7).

David may not have wanted to, or known how to, let God in. It took a truth teller who had access to David to help him deal with his sin.

This is what we need: a community that will speak the truth to us. We need people who will not let us reclassify sin as just an "issue" or a "struggle" and who will know the difference between our frailty and our failure. We neglect true growth and recovery when we try to brush off failure as frailty. So we need a community of people who know us, who love us even in our brokenness, and who will call us to repentance for our failures, for the things we have done and for the things we have left undone.

We need a community that leads us in confession.

When we first started practicing weekly confession with our church family, people found it a bit odd. Why recite a prayer of repentance in the middle of worship? We weren't praying this at special revival services; these were just normal Sunday services. But we became more and more convinced that confession is a missing piece in many of our worship services. Much of contemporary worship music revels in praise but struggles to confess sin. Even many songs that we know and love still fall short. They know how to describe intimacy with God in poetic terms but usually miss the opportunity to name sin as part of the story. Yet is there anything more intimate than the vulnerability of admitting that you're in the wrong?

My wife is a connoisseur of great literature and loves the art of a well-told story. So I've picked up a few things from her along the way. I've been reminded that every great story has a sense of tension and resolution. It occurred to me that it is pretty hard for our church services to tell a story if there is no tension. We were celebrating a resolution—the grace of God—but weren't properly remembering and confessing the tension of our sin.

Worship services are supposed to embody and reenact the gospel. This grand story in its fullness is composed of the tension of human unfaithfulness and the resolution of God's faithfulness. To make our services, in their very shape, tell the gospel story, we had to include a time when we confess our sins. Together. Out loud.

Psalm 51 provides incredibly helpful language when it comes to confession. It contains King David's prayer when he finally and intimately realized the depths of his sin. And so our church began praying a few verses from the psalm each week before communion. It became our rhythm, our liturgy. And it shaped us. We began to notice an intimacy, vulnerability, and honesty we hadn't experienced before. We had found and committed to the tension. Husbands and wives stood next to one another, saying that they had sinned. Parents and children, friends and neighbors, were all on level ground before the cross. It was hard, and it hurt, and sometimes we even cried with one another.

But then something beautiful happened.

Because the tension had become real, the experience of resolution became visceral and powerful. On the heels of confession, we turned corporately to a moment of recognizing God's forgiveness. We asked people to turn to one another and to announce the good news by saying, "Your sins are forgiven in Jesus's name."

Can you imagine the raw beauty and spiritual intimacy of husbands and wives, friends and roommates, brothers and sisters, coworkers and strangers, saying that to one another? It was powerful.

We need a community to lead us in confession. And we need a community to remind us of God's grace.

It's interesting to note that even though Psalm 51 began as David's prayer of individual repentance, over time it became Israel's prayer. It was not just a memory of their king's failure but also language to confess their own unfaithfulness to God.[1] In exile, Israel's consistent and prominent shortcoming was the sin of idolatry. While not everyone participated in idol worship, its effects were contagious, far reaching, and damaging for all the people. Idolatry was often referred to by the prophets as a kind of spiritual adultery. So it makes perfect sense for a prayer of confession after a king's adultery to be the prayer of a nation as it faced the consequences of its sin of spiritual adultery.

Though David initially prayed it as an individual, Psalm 51 is not meant to be merely a private, personal confession. It's in the whole collection of psalms because it became a communal prayer of confession.

THE FACE OF A FAITHFUL GOD

Psalm 51 shows us the power of a true communal confession. First—and perhaps most obviously—confession forces us to face *God*. David wrote, "Against you, you only, have I sinned and done what is evil in your sight" (verse 4). This is quite obviously not true, at least not in the literal sense. Surely David sinned against Bathsheba by using his power as king to summon her to his chamber. Surely David sinned against her husband, Uriah, by taking his wife and then sending him to the front lines where he would be killed. (After all, the Old Testament introduces Bathsheba to us as "the wife of Uriah" as if to set us up to see that she was the victim, not an accomplice, and that Uriah was also one who was sinned against.) And surely David sinned against Israel by failing as the people's king.

No, Psalm 51 is not a way of saying that sin's consequences before God are the only ones that matter. On the contrary, taking the historical account and the psalm together, we see that the point is that *no sin is merely a sin against humanity.* No sin is just a violation of a brother or a sister or a fellow human being. All sins are sins against God. If we have wronged a person, we have wronged that person's Father in heaven. If we have violated creation, we have offended the Creator. Sin has both a horizontal and a vertical dimension. Always. There is no such thing as a victimless crime. There is no way to justify an action because it "isn't hurting anyone." If it goes against the wisdom God has built into His world, if it runs contrary to God's character and purpose, it is a sin against God Himself. Confession makes us face up to that. It is God we must deal with.

But the psalm also shows us *what kind* of God we are dealing with. It reveals this in the opening lines: "Have mercy on me, O God, according to your steadfast love; according to your abundant mercy blot out my transgressions" (verse 1). Confession is rooted in the conviction that God is the God of steadfast love.

Steadfast love. In Hebrew it is one word, one very rich and powerful word: *hesed.* It's the word used to denote God's covenantal love, God's promise of loyalty. It's the word Sally Lloyd-Jones "translates" for children in her brilliant *Jesus Storybook Bible* as God's "Never Stopping, Never Giving Up, Unbreaking, Always and Forever Love."[2] That gets as close as anything I've seen.

And still, God's steadfast love is more.

Earlier in this book we looked at what happened when God revealed Himself to Moses. What Moses heard was not a word about God's justice or wrath—though God most certainly is just and in His justice gets angry. What Moses saw and heard was a glimpse that God *is* in His very essence the God who is gracious, abounding in mercy, full of faithfulness and steadfast love. Because of His love, He cares about justice—about making things that are wrong right again. Because of His love, He gets angry at things that ruin and destroy His world. But all this—His justice and righteousness and anger—are rooted in His love.

David knew this. His appeal to God, his cry for help, his prayer for forgiveness stemmed from his conviction that God is the God of steadfast love.

We forget this. We are prone to think of God as angry or vengeful or capricious. This is how atheist Richard Dawkins saw the "God of the Old Testament." He wrote, "The God of the Old Testament is arguably the most unpleasant character in all fiction: jealous and proud of it; a petty, unjust, unforgiving control-freak . . . megalomaniacal, sadomasochistic, capriciously malevolent bully."[3]

That's not a pretty picture. Nor is it one that is faithful to the Old Testament.

How could God be "jealous" for wanting what is rightfully His as creator? How is it "megalomaniacal" to demand what is not only for His glory but also creation's own good? The story that is often used to demonstrate God's capriciousness is the one where God asks

Abraham to sacrifice Isaac. But that is actually the story that reveals the God of the Old Testament as being *different* from the Canaanite gods who required child sacrifice. He asked Abraham to demonstrate faithfulness in terms Abraham already knew but then used the occasion as an opportunity to show how He was a different kind of God. He does not simply require sacrifice; He provides it.

This is not the place to go blow for blow with Dawkins to counter his depiction of God. The point here is simply that the Old Testament shows us a God who has *always* been the God of steadfast love. God has *always* been the God who forgives our sin and provides the sacrifice. God has *always* been the God who would send Jesus to be the place where mercy and justice meet. God has *always* been the God who would die for us and rescue us.

So when confession forces us to face God, we find the face of the God of steadfast love. This is the power of our communal confession. It leads us back, again and again, to the God of grace.

Facing Each Other at the Table

Confession is not just about sin. Confession is about opening ourselves up to God and to others. So confession is also about vulnerability. And honesty. And humility.

It's a practice that prevents us from keeping our shadows hidden and our frailty forgotten. It isn't just sin that we need to confess; it's our limitations and lack, our weaknesses and warts, our fears and fragility.

Confession turns *brokenness* into *openness*.

But many of us are skilled at giving the appearance of openness while veiling the places of brokenness. We know the art of answering the "How are you?" question with glossy Christianese: "I'm blessed!" What we mean in that situation is "all good!" But what we're actually doing is missing out on a true experience of blessedness by ignoring our brokenness.

Blessedness is not opposed to brokenness. As we saw in the last chapter, we are blessed in our brokenness. If we can begin to believe that down in the depths of our person, maybe we'd become willing to open up with one another.

When we began New Life Downtown as a new congregation of New Life Church, we wanted to find a way to facilitate community throughout the week, outside and alongside Sunday morning. We weren't feeling the need to be clever or to do something wildly unique, but we wanted to design groups in a way that made sense with who we are as a church.

And then it occurred to us: Tables. Meals. This is what we're all about. We gather around the Lord's Table on Sundays and around one another's tables during the week.

So we invited people to start meal groups. The idea was simple, but we wanted it to be clear and easy for everyone to participate. Open up your home, eat together, and pray for one another. Meet. Eat. Pray.

There was something about this that reminded us of the simplicity of Acts 2:42. And we knew there was something counter-cultural about being in one another's homes. In today's drive-through, eat-on-the-run, stare-at-your-phones-during-meals kind of world, the mere act of slowing down and sharing food together is a kind of prophetic resistance.

The response to our approach was stunning. Over the past six years, we have consistently had over 65 percent of our people gather in groups that meet one to two times a month—most often in someone's home—over a meal. And that's just the groups we know about—the ones that are officially in our system, the ones with designated leaders.

There is a hunger for community, for belonging to something like a family. We long for a family that gathers together, eats together, and prays for one another. Our congregation seemed perfectly primed for it. We had a lot of young professionals—single and married—who were living in our area without extended family. They missed their parents, and some had never known the love of an attentive and caring parent. Those who were married—and especially the ones who began having babies—longed for the wisdom and care of others who had accumulated life experience. We also had quite a few empty nesters, couples who were feeling the void after their kids had grown and left home. The simple invitation to open up their homes and meet, eat, and pray became a way for these people to find one another and to get acquainted with those from different generations.

What we discovered was that meal groups weren't just a way to connect people or a clever way of doing small groups. We found something special happening as people slowed down to prepare parts of a meal and brought their dish to a home where their individual contributions became a collective feast. Something happened when people took the time to sit around a table and look one another in the eye, to hear their stories and share their lives. People were finding, some of them for the first time, trustworthy community. Breaking bread became the occasion for breaking open our hearts.

It doesn't take an official church group to experience this. It can begin in small ways with your friends and neighbors. Even if you don't receive communion regularly at your church, the Lord's Table can still be an inspiration to gather around one another's tables. It can be the overflow of grace.

Broken to Be Shared

Luke tells a story of a crowd following Jesus and the disciples even as they were trying to get away (Luke 9). Maybe the disciples were bothered by this. Maybe they had been hoping for a little private retreat with Jesus, some much-needed time with Him. But Jesus, Luke tells us, welcomed the crowd, healed the sick, and was more than happy to teach them about the kingdom of God (see verse 11). By the end of the day, I imagine, the disciples had had enough. "Send the crowd away," they told Jesus (verse 12, CEB). They were tired and hungry and did not want to be responsible for anyone else's needs. They barely had enough for their own needs; the disciples had just five loaves of bread and two fish. No one else had anything to contribute. This was shaping up to be the worst meal group ever. *Who was supposed to get drinks? What about appetizers? Did no one bring the meat?*

Even if they were open to sharing the bread and fish, how could it be enough?

Maybe underneath our exasperation with the needs of others is our own fearful suspicion that what we are and what we have isn't quite enough. *Sure, I may need community, and this community seems to need me, but what do I have to offer? Not much! Maybe they should just go away!*

And yet Jesus wants us to take responsibility for one another. Jesus said to them, just as He says to us, "You give them something to eat" (verse 13, CEB). We cannot walk away from our community. Not because of a lack of compassion, and not because of a feeling of inadequacy. Jesus instructed the disciples to seat the crowd in groups of fifty, and then He took the bread and fish from the disciples, blessed it, broke it, and gave it to the disciples.

This is my favorite thing about the story: Jesus gave it back to the disciples to distribute to the people. He had told His disciples to give the people something to eat. They had protested that there was nothing to give, but Jesus multiplied their meager supplies and then turned back to the disciples and gave them the bread, as if to say, "I meant it: you give them something to eat!" That's the thing about Jesus: He will do the miraculous, but He still wants to involve us. He will do the *multiplication,* but He wants our *participation.*

Jesus says to us, "Place who you are and what you have in My hands. Your broken life. Your story. Your frailty and your failure, your pain and your suffering. Put it in My hands. You'll be surprised by what I can do with it."

In Jesus's hands the small, insignificant, completely inadequate provision became more than enough for thousands. There were basketfuls of leftovers. How is that possible?

Jesus blesses your inadequacy. He gives thanks to the Father for your life, even if you don't. He knows that from your wounds, He can bring healing to others. He knows that out of your emptiness, He can bring fullness. He knows that out of your weakness, He can reveal His strength.

We embody God's grace to one another by offering what we have to Jesus. All it takes is for us to open up. We can share where we've failed in the past, when it is appropriate. We can share where our frailty shows up—maybe as fear or anxiety or loneliness. We can share where the fallenness of the world has touched our lives and left scars. To be sure, there are unhealthy ways of doing this. And there can also be a sort of spiritual voyeurism, where we just want to know the deep, dark stuff in other people's lives. It's like the description given by the character Ron Swanson on the TV show *Parks and Recreation* about Leslie Knope's brief love interest, Justin: "He's a tourist. He visits other people's lives, takes pictures, and leaves. All he wants are the stories."[4] Those are not the sort of people to open up to. We're looking for a trustworthy community. And the goal is not 100 percent transparency either. Vulnerability is never an end in itself; it is a pathway to healing and to intimacy. So we must choose well whom we open up to and how much we share.

But openness is the only way into authentic community. It will involve risk. Any relationship of mutuality and trust does. The church is not a community comprised of those who have something to give and those who need something. The church is not about people who have their lives together and those who are broken. The church is a community of mutuality, where our brokenness becomes a way to open our lives up to one another and allow God to meet us with His grace.

Though I've seen the church fall short of this, I've also seen time and time again the beauty when openness and vulnerability do happen. I know a guy who serves communion at church who can't help but cry every time he looks at the recipients walking through the line and says to them, "The body of Christ, given for you." He knows how the Lord has rescued him from his own struggles with anger and control. And those close to him know it too. That's why their meal group has forged such a deep bond— his openness about past struggles spurred others to be vulnerable as well. And every worshipper who walks through his communion station line might wonder what it is that makes him get so choked up.

Don't despise what you think is a "less than" kind of life. Don't disparage your "not quite enough." Your life in the hands of Jesus can be broken in a new way. Your brokenness can open you up to the grace of God. And your brokenness can open you up to others.

After all, bread that is not broken cannot be shared.

EARTHEN VESSELS

I'm not sure which is easier to do: to open up with someone about the places of sin or to admit the places of frailty in our lives.

I wonder if we can confess our sins to friends with a bit more comfort because of the clarity: *This was wrong.* But to say that we need help, to admit that we've hit our limit, feels weak. There is a kind of shame that accompanies guilt and wrongdoing. But there is a crippling kind of fear that keeps us from community when we think we're the only ones who can't seem to manage. We don't want to be *that* guy or girl or friend who just can't seem to get it together.

Plus, the limits of our own frailty can be fuzzy, so it's easy to keep telling ourselves we're fine.

I know because that's what Holly and I did after having our fourth child. We wanted to be fine. We thought we were fine. We told people we were fine. But we weren't fine. "I feel like I'm drowning," my wife said to me one day. "I just feel so overwhelmed."

Soon it became clear: we needed help.

I picked up the phone and called my dad. My parents were still living in Malaysia at the time. It wasn't the most practical decision, but Holly's parents wouldn't have been able to come so quickly since farm life is difficult to put on hold. When my dad answered in his characteristic way—"How are you doing, son?"—I answered as honestly as I could. "Not very well. We are feeling overwhelmed." Before I could even get out a request for help, he gave the answer: "Do you want me to come?"

I was floored. That was what I was hoping for, though I didn't realize it when I called. My mum was running a school for the community where they served as pastors, and she wasn't able to drop everything and leave. So my dad used airline miles and booked a ticket. Within an hour, it was all settled.

He came and stayed for a month—a whole month. He rocked our baby, Jane, gave us breaks, played with the other three kids, and helped around the house. It was amazing. And it was his presence in our home that changed the atmosphere. My *dad* was there. Everything was going to be okay.

Even writing about this experience, I can feel the emotion of it. He answered before I could even ask. Before I could get out the cry for help, he had already decided to be on his way to us. Isn't that just like the way our heavenly Father responds to us? As the apostle Paul said of Jesus, "God shows his love for us in that while we were still sinners, Christ died for us" (Romans 5:8).

That's what the family of God does for one another: we reveal what the Father is like.

Now, you might think that after a month of my dad's help, everything went back to normal and we were fine. But that is not quite how it went. In fact, things remained challenging for a while. One weekend when I had to travel for a ministry engagement, Jane came down with a double ear infection. Why these things always seem to happen when I'm away, I'll never know. She was about a year old and completely inconsolable. Once again, we asked for help, this time more directly. Holly called some dear friends of ours—Evan and Karen—who were also key leaders in planting New Life Downtown with us.

They didn't hesitate. They came and spent the weekend with Holly, taking shifts through the night to rock baby Jane. They gave up their whole weekend to bear our burdens. It was moments like these that helped us bond. They are like family to us. And it wasn't just them. It was Abby and Lauren and several others who came and spent time with us, lending a hand around the house or just keeping Holly company. The irony here is that we were the pastors of this new congregation—we thought we'd be the ones showing up in other people's homes, serving others who were in need. Yet here we were in need of help. And our community showed up to give us strength.

We may not like the frailty we feel. We may not want anyone else to know how fragile we really are. But we must not be ashamed of the breaks in the earthenware of our lives. It's how we let others in. We have "treasure in jars of clay," the apostle Paul wrote (2 Corinthians 4:7). The treasure is God's grace. And the earthenware is our common, ordinary, often-broken bodies and minds and emotions. The clay is seen in our capacity and limits, our finiteness and weakness. And sometimes the cracks begin to show. Still, the grace of God comes rushing in through those very cracks. And grace comes again and again through the people around us.

In our brokenness we need a community that leads us to confession—of our failure and of our frailty. In our brokenness we need a community of trust and mutuality. And we need a community that embodies God's grace to us. As our brokenness opens us up to the grace of God, that grace arrives through our community.

The Community That Remembers

Sometimes grace looks like remembrance. Sometimes what a community does best is to help us remember and remember *with* us. Maybe the grace in this process is that we become re-membered; the broken pieces are fitted together.

In the mid-1990s an artist named Guenther Demnig began placing "stumbling stones"—*Stolperstein* in German—around Berlin. These were not names of donors or of famous Berliners; these were names of Jewish victims of the Holocaust. For Demnig, a museum doesn't quite do what is most needed. "I think the large Holocaust memorial here [in Berlin] will always remain abstract. . . . With the stumbling blocks . . . suddenly they are there, right outside your front door."

The process is deeply personal and communal. Demnig relies on locals to find out the names of slain Jews in their community and the locations where the victims last lived so the stones can be laid nearby. It makes the horrors real, marking the exact place where a raid led to the torture and death of neighbors.

Hendrik Czeczatka, whose family lived in an apartment where more than forty Jewish residents were taken by the Gestapo, raised the money to have stones placed near the apartment. He explained, "Everybody . . . is responsible, individually, for remembering."

Remembering is important not just to avoid such events again but also to help one another heal. As of 2012 there were more than thirty thousand stumbling stones all across Germany.[5]

We need a community that leads us to confession; we need a community that embodies the grace of God rushing into our frailty; and we need a community that *remembers*. We need a community that remembers our pain, a community that remembers the names of victims and the places where they were oppressed. Remembrance is how we are human together, even in the brokenness of our humanity. In remembrance, we are *re-membered*, and our brokenness begins to be put back together.

And why wouldn't it be that way? For we are made in the image of God. As the famed Holocaust survivor and author Elie Wiesel wrote, "God is God because he remembers."[6] Yes, He does.

Because God is the God who remembers, He is able to hold together both justice and righteousness. The Hebrew prophets, who spoke on behalf of this God, remind us that justice and righteousness belong together. In fact, in the biblical languages the very words are connected. You can even glimpse the connection in English. It is because God is *righteous* that He will set things *right*. It is because God is *just* that He will *justify*. Nowhere is this more clearly displayed than at the cross of Jesus Christ. On the cross Jesus died in solidarity with all who suffer and are oppressed. There He died to take the punishment for the victimizers and the oppressors. For the victim and the victimizer, for the oppressed and the oppressor, Jesus was crucified.[7]

And this flows from God being the God who remembers. God in His remembrance of our pain and suffering went to the cross. God in His remembrance of the violations and the wrong went to the cross. Christ the crucified is a reminder that God remembers.

This remembrance of God is not just seen in the Cross; it is demonstrated in the Resurrection. The Father remembers the Son. The Resurrection was a vindication of that death that brought justice and righteousness together. And the risen Christ is a living reminder that God will bring justice to pass. God will set the world right. God will rectify the wrong. Christ the risen is a reminder that God remembers.

On the eve of His death, on the night that our Lord Jesus Christ was handed over to suffering and death, He took bread and a cup. And He said to do this in *remembrance* of Him. Every time we come to the Lord's Table, we are the community led to confess our sins; we are the community opened up to allow the grace of God to come rushing in; we are the community that remembers. And there at the Table of the crucified and risen Christ, we who are broken become the community that is re-membered.

Movement Three

GIVEN

8

For the Love of Jesus

I sat with my son, four years old at the time, on a small airplane on a late-night flight. As he dozed off to sleep against my arm, my mind began to turn to the purpose of our trip and my heart became heavy. My wife's grandmother had passed away, and her family had asked me to officiate the funeral. That was a huge honor.

My in-laws are from a small farming town in northwest Iowa. Holly's grandparents—both sets, actually—had lived there their whole lives. That community had been the site of nearly every significant moment in their lives. For Gordon and Shirley—Holly's grandparents on her mom's side—the Lutheran church was where milestones were marked. That was the church they had attended and served at for years. It was where their daughters, Roxanne and Coyla, were baptized. It was where Holly's mom, Roxanne, married Bill. It was the church Roxanne and Bill's daughter, Holly, grew up attending. And in a few days, it would be the place where Shirley's funeral would be.

I assumed that the funeral for the family matriarch would have been reserved for the Lutheran pastor to conduct. But the pastor at the time was new to the parish, and in any case, the family wanted me to preach. I was moved by the request. My wife traveled ahead with our youngest, who was about a year and a half at the time. I stayed to preach at our church and then got on a plane later that evening, while my parents—who had now moved to America and were living with us—took care of our two older children.

So there I sat on that tiny airplane, tired and unsure of how to approach the week ahead. I was honored but empty. I was open to the Spirit but near the end of my strength. Truthfully, I felt like *I* could've used a bit of encouragement, yet I was the one tasked with bringing a word of hope.

As I closed my eyes and rested my head against the window, I felt the Holy Spirit whisper, "I am sending you, and I am spending you." I thought instantly of the apostle Paul's words about being "poured out as a drink offering" (Philippians 2:17). Then I started reflecting on the difference between being *drained* and being *spent.* Being drained, in my mind, meant someone was taking something from you, leaving you feeling robbed of energy and strength. Or it meant an accidental or unintentional loss of something, like a bucket that would gradually drain out its contents because of a hole in the bottom.

But the word I heard was *spent,* and being spent somehow seems to be connected to purpose and a choice to intentionally participate. I began turning the words around in my head. What if we are *sent* to be *spent*?

What if when God sends us and we choose to participate in that sending, we can't actually be drained? Maybe in those moments we can only really be spent. I was reminded of the time when Jesus declared that no one *takes* His life from Him; He lays it down (see John 10:18). Jesus's life was poured out, spent with infinite purpose.

That realization changed everything about my approach to that week's events. I went in ready to serve, give, help, listen, and talk—not because someone needed something from me but because God had sent me and God was spending me. Any words, energy, resource, and wisdom I had really belonged to the Lord. He had given it, and He could give it away through me.

In Jesus's hands we become *given*. Every time Jesus took bread, blessed it, and broke it, He *gave* it. Bread is blessed so that it can be given. Bread is broken so that it can be given. Blessedness and brokenness must result in givenness.

We realize our blessedness—that our identity, our calling, and our destiny have come from God and been restored in Christ. We confess our brokenness, opening ourselves up to the grace of God and to the community of grace. But it does not stop there; it cannot stop there. This blessed and broken life was meant to be given away. What was *reclaimed* in God's blessing of us is now *released* in His giving of us.

This bread is *blessed* and *broken* in order to be *given* for the life of the world.

That week in Iowa I experienced the power of this truth in my own story. I was able to honor Shirley's life and point to her legacy in her children, grandchildren, and great-grandchildren. And by God's grace I was able to provide comfort and hope to the family, reminding them of the ancient Christian confession of hope in the final words of the Nicene Creed: "We look for the resurrection of the dead and the life of the world to come." I was able to be the messenger of these words of life only because I embraced the truth that God had sent me in order to spend me. God gave me the gift of being able to see my life as bread in His hands that He wanted to give away for the sake of others.

You may not be able to see it yet, but your blessedness and brokenness is also meant for the life of the world.

BREAD CRUMBS

What if all we have and all we are feel far less than bread and more like crumbs? Could ordinary conversations, simple acts, and consistent kindness make a difference?

My sense from pastoral ministry—from sitting with people through all seasons of life—is that it is usually not selfishness that keeps people from allowing their lives to be used by the Lord. Often it is insecurity or some version of the lie that we are not worth much, that we have nothing to offer, that our lives simply do not matter. Or maybe it isn't selfishness or insecurity that keeps us from being given; perhaps it is simply that we let other activities, lesser loves, and more trivial pursuits crowd out the greatest joy given to us—that of joining God in His work of renewing and restoring all things.

Whatever the reason, maybe the root is the same. We might opt out or miss out on participating in God's work because we haven't seen the grand vista of God's salvation. We think of salvation primarily as something we are recipients of—God showered His grace on us! Yes, of course, this is true. But salvation is also

God's massive plan to put the world back together again. And the people He sets right are the ones He wants to use to set the world right. *Justice* comes through the *justified*. At least, it's supposed to.

God intends for us to be more than recipients of the kingdom; we are to be participants in this arriving reign of God. As ones who have received His grace and have been put right, we are signs of a new creation in the world (see 2 Corinthians 5:17). As ones who work in the Lord so that the work of the Lord will continue, we are agents of the new creation arriving even now (see 1 Corinthians 15:58). Far from having nothing to offer, we have—as the apostle Paul wrote—"this treasure in jars of clay" (2 Corinthians 4:7). Yeah, the pot looks ordinary. But don't be fooled. There is gold inside.

It takes a big view of the gospel to see this truth. That is why we didn't begin this book with a conversation about being given; we began by recovering the blessing. We have been reclaimed and redeemed; our calling has been restored. The mission of God has always been on track. And the mode of that mission has always been human beings, God's image bearers and mission carriers. But where sin tried to derail things and to foreclose on the possibility of our participation, Jesus came to open up the way.

Still, you might feel like there is not much room in your life to give, to sign up to volunteer at church or with a local ministry. Life is already overwhelming. Yet God is not asking us for what we do not have; He is asking for what we do have. So you don't have extra time; you can't take on another commitment. Fine. Consider something you are already doing. How can you turn that over to Him? How can you give Him the day that is already filled with calendar appointments and carpool commitments? Let what you *have* be what you *give.*

My Aunty Yvonne lives in Sri Lanka. When she came to visit last winter, I realized that I hadn't seen her in at least a decade. She is my godmother, a lifelong Anglican, and a fabulous cook.

But there is more to the story than I had realized growing up. My mum told me how she was the first one in their family to become born again—to truly put her faith in Christ and begin following Him. There were five children in all—boys bookending the lineup, with three girls in the middle. As the eldest of the three girls, Yvonne took on a motherly role among her siblings. It seemed the most natural thing for her as the big sister to tell the other siblings about how faith in Christ had become meaningful to her.

But she may not have expected their response. My mother recalled being bothered by my Aunty Yvonne's attempts to get her and my dad to become born again. You may recall that earlier I said my dad became a Christian after meeting my mum in university. But being Christian for them at that time was mostly about going through the motions. It did not mean a total commitment to following Jesus or being in close relationship with Him. My dad said he made fun of my Aunty Yvonne for being so religious, for talking about Jesus and the Bible all the time. *Save that for church,* he thought.

But Aunty Yvonne didn't give up. She prayed. And talked with them. And prayed some more. There was more than birth order or family roles at play; she had found a living faith in a living Christ, and she wanted them to have this kind of faith too.

Finally, through a series of critical events, my parents decided that they needed to be born again. They realized that it was not enough to simply play the part or go to church on Sundays while living as they pleased the rest of the week. They needed to surrender their lives to follow Jesus. Completely. This was what it meant to become different, to be a new creation, to be born again. And so they did.

Shortly thereafter, they decided to go to Canada, where their other sister and her family lived, to try to share the same good news with her. In time, she came to embrace Jesus with a living faith. Her husband, then a cultural Catholic, remained skeptical. For him, checking the boxes was enough; no life change was needed. But years of her loving and faithful presence began to soften his heart. He, too, began following Jesus as the outworking of a deep and personal faith.

This all transpired decades ago, but it was in January 2018 when the three sisters were together in Colorado—together for the first time in years—that the stories began to emerge and converge. The trajectory of our whole family changed because of Aunty Yvonne. Because of her, my parents eventually chose to leave their jobs and their homeland of Malaysia with my sister and me to attend Bible college in Portland, Oregon. Because of Aunty Yvonne's influence and my parents' decision to join her in following Christ, I felt led to study theology in America. And because of all those decisions, I met the love of my life, Holly. And because of that, our four children were brought into the world. But most of all, none of us would be following Jesus today without the persistence and passion of Aunty Yvonne.

Her simple actions led to significant impact. She will tell you, as she told us last year, that she was just a vessel. True. But a vessel carrying a great treasure.

This is what Jesus does with our lives. Small steps of courage and kindness can play a big part in someone's life. Bread in the hands of Jesus becomes more than bread.

And even bread crumbs can lead someone home.

Self-Giving Savior

Jesus is the bread that comes down from heaven, the bread that gives life to the world. Jesus said to the crowd who followed Him, " 'The bread of God is he who comes down from heaven and gives life to the world.' They said to him, 'Sir, give us this bread always.' Jesus said to them, 'I am the bread of life' " (John 6:33–35).

The people who heard Jesus say these things were puzzled. If they were puzzled by these words, they would soon be outraged by His explanation: "I am the living bread that came down from heaven. If anyone eats of this bread, he will live forever. And the bread that I will give for the life of the world is my flesh" (verse 51).

The listeners were stunned. How could He say this? The people would've heard this as a literal instruction. Instead of softening it, or rephrasing it, Jesus upped the ante: "Truly, truly, I say to you, unless you eat the flesh of the Son of Man and drink his blood, you have no life in you. Whoever feeds on my flesh and drinks my blood has eternal life, and I will raise him up on the last day. For my flesh is true food, and my blood is true drink. Whoever feeds on my flesh and drinks my blood abides in me, and I in him" (verses 53–56).

What? Is He insane? Jews can't drink the blood of animals, let alone the blood of humans. Not only did Jesus say it once—that would have been bad enough—but He repeated it three more times. Four times with slight variation, Jesus talked about the necessity of eating His flesh and drinking His blood. I mean, the bread metaphor was confusing, but at least it was more pleasant.

But the point is the same: Jesus came to be consumed; He was sent to be spent. He was the Bread of Life given for the life of the world.

Earlier in the conversation Jesus explained how He, like the manna that came from heaven in Moses's day, had come down from heaven. But Jesus made it clear that unlike manna, which had no volition or choice, He came down from heaven to do not His own will but the will of the one who sent Him (see verse 38). This is a repeated theme in John's gospel—the fully aware, alert, and purposeful Jesus obeying His Father.

Jesus was given for us. It is the most beautiful and true thing we can say; it is the heart of the gospel itself.

To catch just how beautiful it is, we have to confess a mystery we cannot explain. It is the mystery of the Trinity, and specifically, the relationship between the Father and the Son. If we make our distinctions too sharp, we risk sounding like the Father sent the Son against His will or that the Son was forced to go along. Some have even gone so far as to suggest that God acted like an abusive father taking his anger out on his son. That is such an abhorrent misreading.

The verse that is perhaps the best known in the whole Bible frames how we are to see the Cross: "For God so loved the world, that he gave his only Son" (John 3:16).

God *loves* and God *gives*. Why was the Bread of Heaven given for the life of the world? Because God loved the world and gave to it.

Here is where the mystery comes in. Not only does the Father give the Son, but the Son also gives Himself. Because the Son loves the world too. The God who loves the world is none other than the Father, the Son, and the Holy Spirit—the triune God.

Jesus said, "No one takes [my life] from me, but I give it up because I want to" (John 10:18, CEB).

In fact, Jesus said right before this, "This is why the Father loves me: I give up my life so that I can take it up again" (verse 17, CEB). The Father loves the world, and the Father loves the Son. And the Son loves the world, and the Son loves the Father.

So strong is the love between the Father and the Son that there is unity—a union in communion, a communion in the union.

And so it is that the Father's sending of the Son and the Son's giving of Himself are one and the same. They are the same movement, the same motion. The same choreography in the dance. Their giving is not just in harmony; it is in unison.

Jesus knew He was the bread from heaven, given by the Father for the life of the world. And Jesus freely, willingly, gave Himself for us. All this is wrapped up in the strange and beautiful image of bread: it is *blessed, broken,* and *given*.

From Beggar to Bread

If we're honest, there are times when instead of seeing ourselves as bread or even bread crumbs in Jesus's hands, we think of ourselves as beggars, looking for the crumbs. I don't think we'd ever say it that way, but we live that way.

I know because I did.

When I began seeing my spiritual director, he used the picture of a prince who kept leaving his castle to describe the temptations of my soul.

Now, I've got to stop and tell you that I'm not a fan of medieval metaphors. I've got nothing against them, really, but I don't close my eyes and imagine myself as a king riding a white horse into battle. I don't think of my wife as a queen of the castle or our daughters as princesses and our son as a prince. So I was a little leery when my spiritual director started unpacking his metaphor.

But he kept going.

"Glenn, it's like you have a feast prepared for you every night in the castle, but you keep going out and wandering the village begging for bread."

This was striking. *In what way am I begging for bread?* I thought.

"The Father has provided a banquet of His love for you," he continued. "But you think you need to look elsewhere for approval."

I began to think about this, about how I look for online mentions, "likes," and affirmations. I thought about how often I evaluate how I'm being perceived since taking on a lead role at our downtown congregation.

I had begun meeting with my spiritual director because I was afraid of the effect this increased leadership role would have on my ego. There was no crisis, no collapse of faith, nothing that drove me to the decision. Except that sitting in the lead pastor chair of a congregation made me too often the most powerful person in the room. I needed someone off the grid, someone unconnected to our church, to talk with me, pray with me, challenge me, and help me pay attention to all that the Lord was saying and doing.

In our first session I told him how I found myself habitually refreshing the social media apps on my phone, constantly looking for updates or news or things I might be missing out on. He helped me see that my focus had been so much on refreshing these apps that I had neglected practices that refresh my soul.

But now, in this session—one of our early ones—he was putting his finger on something else that was amiss in my life. What was really behind the striving, the stress of being in the public eye, the constant keeping up with everything?

Was I really like a prince leaving the castle looking for bread? Had I begun living like a beggar when I had already been given a feast?

It stuck with me.

Maybe that's you. Maybe that's all of us. Our Father in heaven has lavished His love on us (see 1 John 3:1). His love can satisfy us like the richest of feasts (see Psalm 63:5). And yet we go looking for lesser loves, begging for that which is not bread.

This was what the people of God did when they chased after idols. And God, through the prophet Isaiah, called after them,

> Why do you spend your money for that which is not
> bread,
>   and your labor for that which does not satisfy?
> Listen diligently to me, and eat what is good,
>   and delight yourselves in rich food. (Isaiah 55:2)

We may not be overtly worshipping false gods; we may not even have set up idols of fame or power or money. We may truly have surrendered our lives to the Lord. But we are still prone to wander, to look for sustenance beyond the life-giving source of bread.

The affection, praise, and validation we receive from others is not worthless. Sometimes it *is* the way the Lord meets us with His love. But if we treat it like the Bread of Life, like the core source that satisfies, it becomes "that which is not bread." The more we grasp for it, the tighter we hold on to it, the faster it turns to sand, slipping from our hands. We have to learn to hold loosely the praise of others, the affection from people, knowing that we have a feast that awaits us in the Father's house. It is always there.

As the Father said to the older son in the story of the prodigal son in Luke 15, "Everything I have is yours!" (verse 31, CEB).

Stop for a moment. Open the eyes of your heart and behold. Everything the Father has is ours. Christ the Son is ours. The Father's love has been lavished on us. We have become children of God and heirs of this glorious inheritance (see Romans 8:16–17).

Only when we feast on the Father's love do we stop living like beggars.

And here's the thing: *We cannot be bread that is given for the world if we live like beggars chasing after that which does not satisfy.*

GIVEN FOR THE LOVE OF JESUS

From being loved, we love. It is in being beloved that we become love. And love gives. Maybe it is in the act of giving that love is most manifest.

But what is the object of our love? Whom do we love in order to allow ourselves to be given? Or what do we love in order to become given?

The answer seems obvious: the person you are serving, the one to whom you are given. If your life is to be given for your children, then it is the love for your children that leads you to that place. If your life is to be given in service of the poor, then it is the love for the poor that leads to that givenness.

Yes, that is the obvious answer. But I think it's wrong.

At least, it's incomplete. And, frankly, insufficient. It's not enough to sustain us, to carry us through the dark nights and the lonely hours. It won't push us through the pain and the hurt we've experienced from the very ones we were trying to help.

If you don't believe me, ask the apostle Peter.

After the Resurrection, Peter returned to fishing. Think about it: He ran to the tomb. He saw that it was empty. He was, most likely, with the other disciples when Jesus appeared to them. He may have been there when Thomas placed his hands on Jesus's scars. And still he went back to his old livelihood.

Maybe Peter felt he had lost it all that night when he denied knowing Jesus. Maybe Peter was too confused about what the Resurrection really meant. Maybe whatever it meant, Peter was too covered in shame for it to matter. He might as well try to just live a quiet life, a smaller story.

But John 21 describes how Jesus found Peter and reenacted the scene of their first encounter, the first time Jesus called Peter to follow Him.

"Cast the net on the right side of the boat," the voice called out from the shore. Peter knew he had heard that voice before. But it was John who recognized Him.

"It is the Lord!" John said to Peter.

It might have been John who recognized Jesus first, but it was Peter who responded—and responded radically. Peter threw on his robes and swam to shore, leaving the other disciples to drag the fish—a big haul of fish—behind the boat to shore.

After their breakfast on the beach, Jesus asked Peter a simple question, a heart-piercingly simple question: "Do you love me more than these?"

Who were "these"? The other disciples? Did Jesus mean, "Is your love for Me greater than their love for Me?" Or did He mean, "Is your love for Me greater than your love for the disciples?" We can't be sure. Yet Peter's answer acknowledged that whichever way the question was intended, Jesus already knew the answer.

"Yes, Lord; you know that I love you," Peter replied.

"Feed my lambs," Jesus responded.

This exchange continued two more times, with minor variances. There has been much scholarly and theological exploration of the nuances and shifts in word choices between the Savior and His disciple. But the main point is that Jesus was reinstating Peter. He was reaffirming Peter's purpose, calling, and destiny. The three repetitions of the question are meant to correspond to Peter's three-fold denial.

The most significant bit, however, is the one hidden in plain sight.

In this restorative, call-renewing conversation, Jesus asked Peter, simply, repetitively, and piercingly, "Do you love *me*?"

Not "Do you love the sheep?"

Not "Do you love the food?" meaning "My teachings."

Not "Do you love yourself?"

Not "Do you love the purpose and mission?"

The question was simply "Do you love *me*?"

In another gospel account of Peter's first call, Jesus said to Peter, "Follow me, and I will make you [a fisher] of men" (Matthew 4:19). You might say that first call was about a *purpose.* In essence, Jesus said, "Peter, I'll lift you from a life that is going nowhere. I'll sweep you up into the greatest story of all. I'll give you a role in the kingdom of God arriving on earth as it is in heaven. I'll make you a participant and not just a recipient." That is, after all, what it means to be *given.*

But it isn't the love of being given that leads to our givenness. It isn't the love of a purpose that can sustain us. In the end that was not enough to keep Peter faithful. The love of a calling will never keep you from falling.

If Peter's first call was about a *purpose,* this second call—this renewal of destiny and identity—was about a *person.* "Peter, do you love *me?*"

Do you love Jesus? Do you love Jesus above all else? Lesser loves may lead you to begin following Jesus or even to enter into vocational ministry. But these cannot sustain you. The love of meaning or mission or purpose or the church will not keep you surrendering and serving. Only a deep and abiding love for Jesus can do that.

It is our love for Jesus that leads us to surrender to *Him.* And it is Jesus who gives us away for others. We surrender out of love for Him. And when we surrender, we find ourselves not needing to beg any longer. Our surrender makes us bread in the hands of Jesus.

He sends us and spends us because of His love for us and for the world. And the sending is sweeter than you could have ever dreamed or imagined. This is how we become given for the life of the world.

For One Another

The church in Carthage had been through hell, but things were about to get worse. It was the year AD 251, and a deadly plague was ravaging their city at the western edge of North Africa, in modern-day Tunisia. People were panic stricken and began fleeing as quickly as they could. And the Christians were in no position to help. They were dealing with a crisis of their own.

Two years earlier, the Roman emperor Decius had begun requiring all people to offer sacrifices to the Roman gods. North Africa was a prominent part of the Roman Empire at that time, and Decius worried that the Christians throughout the land were bringing ill fortune upon everyone else.

Religion in the ancient world and in the centuries after it was not like it is today—an essentially private practice and personal choice. No, religion was the shared system of beliefs and practices that bound people together, creating solidarity, and permeated all of life. The historian of early Christianity Robert Louis Wilken wrote, "Piety toward the gods was thought to insure the well-being of the city, to promote a spirit of kinship and mutual responsibility, indeed, to bind together the citizenry."[1]

That is why the gospel and the church formed by it in the first century were a threat to Roman society. It undercut the way old bonds of solidarity were forged.

In addition to the sociological dynamics of shared practices and solidarity, there was also quite a bit of superstition in the world around the early church. If a segment of society was not making offerings to the gods, the gods might get angry. A disease may come or calamity may befall a community. It was risky to have an ever-increasing corner of a city abstaining from offering sacrifices to the gods.

It was well known that Christians refused to pray to the gods or participate in the cult of emperor worship. The only group that had been granted an exemption from such practices had been the Jews, and even then only because of a long-standing agreement with Roman rulers. But the Christians were relatively new to the scene. They weren't quite Jewish, which meant they weren't protected under the Romans' agreement with the Jews, and they weren't like the Romans, who called on a collection of various gods. Christians were in the pressured middle space. Decius's requirement to offer sacrifices to the gods seemed like the right thing to do in the interest of what we might call "national security." Christians who refused to participate were persecuted and perceived as a nuisance at best and a threat at worst.

In his book *The Patient Ferment of the Early Church,* Alan Kreider wrote about the hardship many churches experienced from this focused persecution.[2] A few Christians were even executed. Some Christians showed what we may say were lapses in their faith by signing documents affirming they had completed the necessary deeds to honor the gods; other believers remained faithful and endured great pain.

By the year 250 the persecution had for the most part come to an end, but the unity in the church had endured significant damage. Those who had remained faithful and had suffered because of it did not think well of those who had either performed the sacrifices or signed documents saying they had. Why should those who had lapsed in their faithfulness be allowed to worship alongside courageous Christians who had followed in the way of the suffering servant, Jesus Christ?

Then there was the strain between Christians and their pagan neighbors who had betrayed them. Many Christians had been reported by these neighbors, and some had even been open about it. There was no way around it: these people were not neighbors to be loved but enemies to be feared.

So when the plague hit the next year, people were terrified. The fabric of the community had been torn. And now people were vomiting, suffering with severe diarrhea, and running high fevers. Those infected were often carried out into the streets and left to die. Those not infected often fled the city. The sick and dying begged for pity from those passing by, but to little effect. These were like scenes from a postapocalyptic movie. How would the church in Carthage survive?

The bishop of Carthage was a man named Cyprian. He had been born to wealthy parents and had been trained as a lawyer.

During his law career he converted to Christianity and experienced a powerful transformation during his baptism. He was appointed bishop just a few years later. Though he had gone into hiding during the persecution in AD 249, he came to understand his role as a leader in the city.

As the plague ravaged the community, Bishop Cyprian called a special meeting of the Christians in Carthage. We don't know much about what happened at the gathering or even where they met. But we do know what the bishop said to his flock. He asked them to respond in "a way that was marked by courage and patience."[3] These qualities, Cyprian said, would demonstrate the difference between Christians and pagans. Cyprian, unlike the pagan leaders and philosophers, was uninterested in *why* the plague had occurred; he was concerned with *how* Christians should respond. Cyprian reminded listeners of what Jesus said in the Sermon on the Mount: that God sends rain on the just and on the unjust.

The first main point of his sermon was that Christians should show mercy the way God their Father shows mercy. He reminded them that Christians, as children of the merciful God, have a long tradition of creating "an organization, unique in the classical world, that effectively and systematically [cares] for its sick."[4]

His second point may have made his listeners squirm. He called on them to imitate God not only by showing mercy but also by loving their enemies. Their care should not be restricted to Christians only, because Christ had called all His followers to love their neighbors *and* their enemies.

As hard as it may have been after the terrifying time of persecution, the Christians in Carthage took their bishop's words to heart.

They cared for one another, even the people they struggled to embrace in their own congregations. Their love spilled out into the world as they cared for the "outsiders" who were suffering.[5]

And it changed everything.

The sociologist Rodney Stark speculates that basic care, such as providing food and water, resulted in a much higher ratio of Christian survivors to pagan survivors. Moreover, because Christians cared not only for other Christians but also for pagans, the surviving pagans were eyewitnesses to the courage and compassion of the Christians.[6]

The people of the church in Carthage allowed themselves to be given, for one another and for the world around them. And because of it, Christianity spread and the church grew.

PARTIES AND PATIENCE

I'm not much of an outdoorsman, but because we live in Colorado, we feel it is our duty to go camping at least once each summer (though sometimes we have left our duty undone). We acquired a nice tent and some cool gear from our local REI, and its mere presence in our garage prompts us to make use of our investment and venture out into nature.

Most of the time we go with friends who are veteran campers. By the time the tents are set up, the sun is slowly dipping behind the mountains and it's time to get a fire going. Dinner under the stars sounds like it should be enchanting and magical. But with all our children—usually about eight to twelve among our families—it's often quite chaotic. It doesn't help that I'm the adult who is most prone to stress due to catastrophizing—you know, I imagine the worst catastrophe that could occur in any setting. A child is going to get burned from the fire or disappear into the pitch-black woods. A bear is going to smell meat and invade our campsite.

But I digress. Camping meals require great patience. For one thing, there is only one fire. So there are only so many pans you can fit over the flame. And then there's the reality that cooking over an open fire can take a long time because the heat may be uneven. Or you may char a hot dog or two because flames leap up unpredictably. This is all complicated by the number of people trying to share a meal together. The adults will wait for the kids to eat first, and by the time the grown-ups finally sit down to eat, the kids are hungry again. A roll may fall on the ground. Ketchup will get on someone's shirt. Drinks will be spilled. Hands might get scalded from getting too close to the fire.

Anytime a dozen or more gather for a shared meal in one place—*any* place—patience is required. But when there's only one fire for everyone to gather around, to cook their food on, and to gain heat from, you *really* need patience.

Now think back to the church in Carthage and the way they showed patience with one another and with the suffering of their pagan neighbors. They were like a people gathered around one fire, learning to deal with the mess and immaturities of such a community. The story of their compassion is striking but not surprising. It is, as Bishop Cyprian had told his people, what Christians do. Moreover, it is what Christians have been *formed* to do. The book of Acts records that the first Christians "devoted themselves to the apostles' teaching and the fellowship, to the breaking of bread and the prayers" (Acts 2:42). A few verses later, the phrase appears again: "And day by day, attending the temple together and breaking bread in their homes, they received their food with glad and generous hearts" (verse 46).

Breaking bread together was a central part of what the first Christians did. It was as if the gathering around the Lord's Table became a pattern for them as they gathered around one other's tables. It wasn't just another practice. The sharing of bread together formed them to be people who shared their lives with one another. It formed them to be people who shared God's mercy with one another. It formed them to be people who shared everything they had received with one another. The breaking of bread made them a one-another kind of people.

Early Christians had developed the habit of patience through their worship and practices. They had become a people that learned to take the long view. They weren't after quick dramatic impact; they weren't trying to make big splashes; they didn't even launch evangelism campaigns. Instead, it was their steadfast witness, their patient persistence, their "long obedience in the same direction"[7] that eventually led others to be drawn to them.

Patience may not seem like the kind of virtue that would result in the conversion of pagans. But think about it for a minute. It was the patience of the early Christians that led them to embrace a different sexual ethic than the culture around them—they waited for marriage; they did not have sex outside of marriage; and some committed to celibacy. It was patience that helped them resist the normal temptations toward greed and coercive power. The early

Christians never compelled others to believe as they did. In fact, we would say they often made the process harder for pagans to convert! In the end, it was patience that fortified them to endure suffering and persecution because they believed that the future could be entrusted to God. It was the patience of the early Christians that allowed them to resist revenge and violence. Patience was the fruit of hope, and hope was strengthened by their patience.[8] They learned this patience through the practice of shared meals together.

As the gospel spread into predominantly Gentile communities, there were divisions that had to be overcome. Roman society was highly stratified; there were divisions and separations, lines that one did not cross. No setting made this more apparent than feasts. The poor and powerless would never have been allowed in or invited to a feast. Banquets were thrown by the powerful for the powerful to display their power. But that was not what Christians did. In Carthage, for example, Christians would gather for an evening meal in someone's home as part of their weekly worship. Present among them were people who had been pushed to the margins of society. But they were never made to feel that way here. At the table with Christians, they were welcome. They were fed. And they were allowed to speak. They were treated with dignity and worth, recognized for having gifts to offer and contributions to make.

Where did the Christians in Carthage learn patience with one another? Where did they form the habit of deferring to one another? Where did they practice the art of showing mercy and hospitality to one another?

At the Lord's Table, of course.

These were people who had been formed by the breaking of bread. So when the time came to allow their lives to be given like broken bread for one another and even for their enemies, they had been prepared.

TABLE HOSPITALITY IS HEALING INCLUSIVITY

I don't think the church in Carthage should be considered a one-time shining example, an aberration from the norm. I have been a witness to the way coming to the Lord's Table forms us to prepare a table for others. I've seen the way the Table forms us to be a hospitable people in our own community at New Life Church.

Shortly after planting our downtown congregation, Bobby, one of our pastors who works with our local outreach, received a call from a family to bring food to a pregnant woman who had no housing. Bobby picked up food from the New Life food pantry and went to the home where Fiona had been sleeping on a couch. It was a rough situation, and Bobby and his wife, Brooke, began to pray about how to help.

Two months later Fiona showed up at New Life Downtown, and Bobby and Brooke recognized her. They learned that Fiona was pregnant with twins and had no place to live. She had come from a decent home, though finances had always been in short supply. As a young adult, she began dating a guy who had experienced considerable hardship. Both of them started down a road of destructive drug use and soon found their lives unraveling. When Fiona came to the church that day, her boyfriend had just gotten out of jail and they were living on the streets, though it was uncertain if he would remain in her life.

Bobby and Brooke are two of the most pure-hearted followers of Jesus I know. They are not easily encumbered by material pursuits or distracted by institutional trappings. They love Jesus and people—wholeheartedly and unreservedly. And so, that very Sunday, they made the decision to invite Fiona and her boyfriend to move in with them.

After about a week they knew they needed a long-term solution, at least for Fiona, especially with the twins arriving soon. When Brooke, who was on our downtown church staff at the time, told me about Fiona, I wondered how we could help. We didn't really have the resources to do much. Nor did we have much experience on what long-term support would look like. This was before we had opened Mary's Home (an outreach of Dream Centers of Colorado Springs)—an apartment complex for single moms who have found themselves in need of housing, career counseling, and more.

But we knew we had many compassionate people in our congregation. Bobby and Brooke organized a dinner for my wife and me to meet with a couple who had begun attending our congregation and had expressed a desire to help a homeless single mom. Dave and Hayley hosted us in their newly remodeled downtown home, a home they had wanted to make available to us for gatherings with our volunteers and other activities. That evening, over a meal, we talked about the possibility of Fiona living in their guesthouse, a nice freestanding cottage in their backyard. It would be a risk. None of us really knew Fiona. None of us knew if she would ever be able to support herself and her twins. And none of us knew how much her boyfriend would be in the picture. But something was stirring in us. We felt that the Lord was giving us a chance early in the life of our congregation to decide what kind of community we would become. Would we be only an inward-facing community, or would we learn to extend our hands outward? These habits form early in a church.

Dave and Hayley, to their everlasting credit, made a massive decision that night. They decided to take a risk. These are the moments when we wish for a burning bush like Moses saw or a voice from heaven or some clear sign that will sustain us on the days when it feels like we made a terrible choice. The kind of faith that acts on courage and compassion over clarity and certainty is a kind worthy of honor in my book. What I didn't know until only recently was that before Dave and Hayley moved into their home, God had spoken to them, telling them they would house a single mom in their backyard cottage. In fact, God had given Hayley a picture of a woman's face—a face Hayley recognized later as Fiona's.

Fiona moved into the guesthouse that fall. And the church rallied around her. Women from the church threw her a baby shower, gifting her with car seats, strollers, cribs, and more. She was blown away.

As the months went on, Fiona's boyfriend would show up randomly and disappear unexpectedly, creating more chaos for her. The two of them had a hard time staying clean, even after the twins were born. Dave and Hayley had to set boundaries for what could and couldn't take place in their guesthouse. Eventually, Fiona moved out, and the road remained bumpy. Her climb toward stability faced many obstacles. Sometimes people from the church were able to help; other times we could not. Sometimes she and the twins showed up at church; sometimes months would go by without seeing them. But through it all she knew we were eager to help. There were people she could call, friends who would be with her. Lately, the journey has been more settled than not.

On the Sunday after Easter in 2018, I received word that Fiona had come ready to baptize the twins. I wasn't sure at first. Her kids were younger than I preferred for baptism, but I knew we were also baptizing their cousins that day. Through Fiona's own faith her brother came to know the Lord in the midst of his own tragedy and crisis. So Fiona and her twins attended the baptismal class that morning. And around eleven thirty on April 8, 2018, we baptized them along with a dozen others, including my own son.

I stood in front of the church and shared just a bit of Fiona's story. Despite the adversity she has faced, Fiona now has a stable job and good housing, and she is clean and sober. I didn't say all that in front of the church, but she told me I could have shared it all. "The church has been everything to us," she said. And then it hit me: *this* is what it means to be the family of God. We who were undeserving and yet have been welcomed to the feast can welcome others to come. We who have been given a seat at the Table of the Lord can prepare a table for others to find Jesus as well.

And when we are welcomed at Jesus's Table, we begin to be different. Don't miss this about the way Jesus welcomed people: inclusion in the community is never without helping to make a person whole. Luke's gospel recounts story after story of Jesus finding the outcast and the outsider—the leper and the lame, the blind and the beggar. There was another community in Jesus's day that set themselves apart as they awaited the kingdom of God. They were the Qumran community. But they explicitly excluded disabled people—those who were lame, blind, deaf, and dumb—so as to remain pure. They wanted to be pure enough for the Messiah to spring from their midst.[9] But Jesus healed all kinds of people with all kinds of infirmities. He did this as a sign that when the kingdom of God comes, it is not simply *inclusion* but a *healing inclusion* that results. It is not a blanket inclusivity like our modern notions of acceptance or tolerance. Rather it is, as New Testament scholar and historian N. T. Wright wrote, a "radical and healing inclusivism"—one that healed what was disoriented, disordered, and broken.[10]

Fiona's journey was not a continual upward trajectory toward a stable life. There have been many ups and downs. And despite our best efforts, people were hurt and messes were made along the way. Yet God took our plain old offering, the "bread" of being the church, and blessed it, broke it, and gave it for Fiona and her children and for their uncle and cousins. Table hospitality became a healing inclusivity for her and her family.

GIVING BEGETS GIVING

There is a kind of cycle to givenness. Giving begets more giving.

The self-giving of God generates our own self-giving to others. It seems to be this way by God's design. Does this make God's giving not quite pure? Does a true gift need to be one with no expectation of return?

The practice of gift giving around the world is varied and

diverse. When a friend brought food to my family's home when I was a child, it was a gift that initiated a cycle of giving. In Malaysia, as in many cultures in the East and in the Global South, reciprocity is an unspoken value. You cannot simply receive a gift; you have to give one as well.

Now, to Western minds, this seems silly at best, coercive at worst. *Isn't that manipulative? Why give to get? Shouldn't you give with no strings attached?*

But this is a failure to comprehend the way reciprocity works. Reciprocity is not giving to get. It is a way to reinforce a relationship.

Actually, we discover this early in life. If a friend lets you borrow a toy, you feel you should let that friend have a turn with yours. If you get invited to a friend's birthday party, you will probably give an invitation to your party as well. Returning the favor is a social instinct.

But it doesn't always transfer to the practice of gift giving. The New Testament scholar John Barclay traced the anthropology of gift giving in the ancient world in an effort to locate the apostle Paul's notion of grace (the Greek word simply means "gift") within its cultural context.

He made some fascinating observations. For one, Barclay noted that "gifts [were] generally given in order to create or reproduce social bonds; they foster mutuality, and for this reason [were] typically neither unilateral nor anonymous." They were not a one-way donation. Furthermore, the unofficial "rules of reciprocity raise the expectation of return," though not in a legal sense. A return was expected even when the giver and the recipient were not of equal status. A rich man may give to a poor man, and a return of some sort would be expected of the poor man even if the return would likely be different from the gift both in "quantity and kind."[11]

Basically, if someone gave you something, you needed to give him something in return. This was done not as a repayment and not necessarily because the person was expecting it but because that was how you showed him that the gift meant something to you and that *the person* mattered to you. It didn't matter if he was wealthy and didn't need anything; it didn't matter if you could never match the quality of his gift. It was the gesture of reciprocating that reinforced the relationship.

Much of this custom of reciprocity in gift giving was undone, perhaps unwittingly, some five hundred years ago by the German reformer Martin Luther. Let me explain. Luther was so determined to rid people's minds of the notion of "works righteousness" that he talked very little about Christians reciprocating God's grace—living differently because of the way God had saved them.

This doesn't mean Luther didn't believe in living differently; he simply didn't want to connect that behavior to any kind of "service to God" in case people might slip into old habits and start thinking they could impress God or earn some reward from Him.

A century later philosopher Immanuel Kant took Luther's theological interpretation of grace and universalized it to refer to the way humans ought to give to one another as a matter of duty, not out of any sort of relational reciprocity.

This thinking is a long way from the Jewish world of the Bible. In the Old Testament, love for one's neighbor was a way to demonstrate one's love for God. If God showered His blessings on your crop or livestock, giving you abundance, you demonstrated thanks to God by caring for those who had less. The care of the poor was a way to return God's blessings to Him. "Whoever is generous to the poor lends to the LORD, and he will repay him for his deed," says Proverbs 19:17. This was why Jesus could say, generations later, that "as you did not do it to one of the least of these, you did not do it to me" (Matthew 25:45).

What Luther did with good intentions and understandable pastoral motivations, Kant took one step further, and the result is a view of gifts and giving that is vastly different from the approach in the Bible. Those of us who don't live in the East or Global South may have to work harder to change our view. Gifts are meant to provoke giving; generosity is meant to generate more generosity.

At the heart of the gospel is grace, a gift that provokes giving. God is gracious. He gives good gifts, even to those who do not deserve it. And those who receive God's good gifts are to return them *upward* in praise and *outward* in service.

Grace follows the pattern of reciprocity common to gift giving in the ancient world, but with two key differences. First, God's grace is given to the *unworthy*. No one is fit to receive what God has lavished on us. Second, God's grace is meant to generate reciprocity in a wider circle, benefiting even those who are outside. Grace begets grace. Giving begets giving. Or as Jesus said, "Freely you received, freely give" (Matthew 10:8, CSB).

The givenness of Jesus, the bread of life, makes our givenness as the church, the body of Christ, possible. And so the church—that community formed by the givenness of Christ—comes to be a people who are given for one another and for the sake of the world.

The Christians in Carthage knew this, even if they didn't like it. They knew they had no real choice as followers of Jesus but to welcome back into the community repentant Christians who had faltered in their allegiance to Christ during the period of persecution. They were to care for the sick, regardless of how they had behaved during the persecution. They were to show the kind of mercy to their enemies—the neighbors who had betrayed them—that God in Christ had shown to them.

This grace is to produce more grace. The generosity of God is meant to form a generous community. The great gift of God makes us a given people.

IO

For the Life of the World

Jesus called Himself the bread that "came down from heaven" and announced that His body was given "for the life of the world" (John 6:51). If we as the church are to see ourselves as Christ's body here in the world, then part of what it means to be given is to be in the world for its own good.

But what if the world does not want us or even view Christians as being "good"? How can we collectively, as Christians in our communities, try to bring life to the world when the world doesn't think it needs it? So far, we've talked about the personal dimension and the communal dynamic of being given—what leads us to that posture and what it looks like in a congregation. But what does being given look like in our culture at large, especially a culture where Christianity is not always welcome?

Before we can answer that, we must look closely at our world and how its attitudes toward faith have changed. The Malaysia of my childhood was a melting pot of Southeast Asia, bringing together the languages, cultures, and religions from many countries in that corner of the world. Take language as an example. Most Malaysians—that moniker itself refers to a nationality and not an ethnicity—speak at least two languages. That's because one of the legacies left by the British Empire is that English is spoken at least in the cities and major towns. But after the British left, public education had to be taught in Malay by law. If you were a Chinese Malaysian, you may have spoken Cantonese in your home, Malay in school, and English around town with your friends.

The cultural fusions are even more interesting. In addition to the English language, schools, and a parliamentary form of government, the British also left behind a fascination with their way of life. My maternal grandfather, for example, insisted on ordering his shoes and cuff links from a shop in London. Growing up, I saw how East and West blended together, nowhere more clearly than at the dinner table. I grew up eating pork chops with Chinese chili sauce and roast chicken with curry powder, usually served with a side of rice.

When it came to religion, there was a mosque down the street from our home. Two doors down, a bright-red Buddhist altar hung on the wall by the front door, with a holder for incense sticks. Many of the relatives on my dad's side of the family are Hindus, and visits to their homes meant staring with childhood curiosity at the shrine room on the main level closed off by a wall of bead strings hanging from the ceiling to the floor.

I grew up around Muslims, Buddhists, and Hindus. I went to school with them, played around the neighborhood with them, and swam at the health club with them. I ate at restaurants, played at the park, rode the bus, and shopped at the mall with people who believed deeply in these ancient religions. Before I knew what religious pluralism was, I was steeped in it.

Major cities around the world have begun to resemble the kind of multilingual, multicultural, multireligious world I knew as a child in Malaysia. Pluralism—of all kinds—is the urban and increasingly suburban norm.

Ironically, it is precisely this religious pluralism converging in a common space that is giving rise to what some are calling a new "secular age." By this they do not mean an age where no one believes in God. That would be a subtraction story—a tale of how culture eradicated God from its consciousness. Rather, as described by Oxford philosopher Charles Taylor, it is an age when belief is contested, when faith is no longer the default position.[1] In the past, especially in America, we may have assumed that most people thought they *should* believe in God but just got caught up with work or decided to go sow their wild oats or whatever the case may be. Today, few, if any, start from that premise. And if one does believe in God, that belief is often challenged, questioned, or opposed. A person might ask, "Why do you assume there is a God? Why do you assume that faith is necessary? Why should we actually believe this way?" Religious belief is now contested because of the religious pluralism in the global village in which we now live.

That may seem like a strange thing to say. If more religions are coexisting in the same space, why would that result in religion itself being contested or questioned? Let's take American communities as an example. It used to be that the only people we knew in our town were people more or less like us: we all had the same rough definition of goodness, and we shared the notion that "good people" go to church on Sunday. Now people live in the same kinds of homes, drive the same kinds of cars, buy groceries at the same place, and have lives that *look* the same, but their belief systems are very different. Some might adhere to different religions, and some might worship the subtle gods of materialism and individualism. Yet it seems that everyone is still in pursuit of "the good life," even if the definition of goodness is far more diverse than before. The surface of our lives seems the same even while the convictions and religious beliefs at the core are radically different.

We are left to wonder if faith actually has any bearing on the quality of life or the way we live. If a person may have the same quality of life as another while believing radically different things, then maybe religious belief doesn't matter. We see Christians whose lives have fallen apart and non-Christians whose lives seem to be working; we see churchgoing people exhibit greed and selfishness and Muslims who are kind and sacrificial. Our culture concludes that faith is just a private matter or a personal decision. As long as our communities are safe and thriving and people are not being hindered in their pursuit of their own vision of an authentic life, then it really doesn't matter. So you see, it is religious pluralism that has ushered in a kind of secularism, an indifference to religion.

In fact, more than simply being contested in a post-9/11 world, religion is now assumed to be a threat to a flourishing society. The prevailing sense is that we can figure out how to do neighborhoods and soccer games and orderly societies and that we don't really need religious people interfering with this. Not only is faith irrelevant, but it actually may be an *obstacle* to the American dream.

Faith is irrelevant at best or dangerous at worst. We live in a world in which believers are tempted to doubt and doubters are tempted to believe.[2] Things are more challenging than we might like, but there is an opportunity in our midst.

Welcoming the Strangest Stranger

Luke tells a story of Jesus's encounter with two disillusioned people. From this story we can learn something about the way *He* was given that illuminates a pathway for *us* to be given in our secular, cynical age.

In the final meal story in Luke's gospel, we meet two downcast disciples. In fact, this may be putting it too lightly. They were disillusioned and distressed, confused and disoriented. *How could this have happened?*

This was not where they saw the story going. As the other gospels describe it, Jesus, the person the disciples had thought was the Messiah, had ridden into Jerusalem the way the prophets had envisioned a revolutionary doing so—on a colt, with a cheering crowd waving palm branches and chanting, "Hosanna!" The mob in Jerusalem that day was there for a revolution. Decades earlier, Judah Maccabee had done the same, and the palm branch became a symbol of God restoring the kingdom to Israel through his victory. The festival of Hanukkah marks this brief but triumphant period in Israel's life.

So when Jesus came to Jerusalem, His followers were sure *this was it*. The donkey was not a picture of humility; instead, it was the well-known symbol of victory. A revolution was coming, and they would be victorious! Jesus would overthrow the Romans and restore the kingdom of God on earth through Israel.[3]

The disciples had high kingdom expectations, and their vision of how it would arrive had been shaped not only by the great Hebrew prophets but also by events in recent memory. Then a shocking thing happened. Jesus went to Jerusalem . . . and got arrested! When soldiers came for Him with swords and clubs, He didn't even put up a fight. And not because the disciples weren't ready. The story, the way Luke tells it, is that when they came to arrest him, one of them asked, "Lord, shall we strike with the sword?" And before Jesus could tell him no, this person—another gospel writer tells us it was Peter—cut off the ear of the high priest's servant. Jesus hadn't authorized this, and instead He acted to reverse it. Jesus healed the man's ear, right there in front of the soldiers (see Luke 22)!

Things went from bad to worse. Jesus was severely mocked and beaten. The disciples watched from places of hiding as He was brought before Pilate and then before Herod and then back to Pilate. They must have heard the crowds jeer at Him, calling for the convicted criminal Barabbas to be released instead of Jesus. The crowd's anger was fueled, no doubt, by their feeling of being duped. Maybe the disciples wondered why they had invested so much hope in this would-be Messiah. Why had they given up their careers and left their homes to follow Him? What had it all been for, now that they saw Him captured and beaten? What kind of Messiah was this? They may have wanted to join in with the crowd too. *I'd rather free a Jewish criminal than a failed Messiah.*

They saw Him carry a cross, stumbling every few steps, up to the place where He would be crucified. Was there a more humiliating way to die? No—not then and maybe not since. One man emerged from the crowd to carry the cross for Jesus, but what good would that do? That would only postpone the inevitable, the shameful disgrace of a crucified Messiah.

Then it happened: Jesus was crucified between two thieves. This was too much. Had they really put their trust, their hopes, and the longing and aching of a nation in *this* man?

Still, they stayed and watched the whole thing.

On the way to Emmaus, two disciples—if not among the twelve, then among the many—hung their heads and hid their tears. Unable to quench the fire of their disappointment, they turned on each other, arguing and debating about the Messiah.

At that moment Jesus Himself "arrived and joined them on their journey" (24:15, CEB).

That's amazing, isn't it?

Jesus joined the disappointed and the disillusioned in their journey. He didn't say "Come over here" or "Come to Me" or "Come follow Me." No, that was all well and fine the first time. But not this time. Not when faith had been shattered, when hopes had been badly broken. No, when we are too weak, too broken to come to Jesus, He *comes to us.* He Himself joins us on the journey.

Yet He waits for us.

After asking them what they were talking about and then acting ignorant about the events in Jerusalem the previous three days, Jesus began to explain to them from the law and the prophets how it had been prophesied that the Messiah would have to suffer and then be raised up (see verse 27). They had been reading the Scriptures wrong. Before they could recover from that paradigm shift, Jesus went on to another: He showed them how the Scriptures spoke of *Him.* Can you imagine that conversation?

Then, when they reached Emmaus, Jesus decided to act as if He was continuing on the road, just to see if they were curious enough, awake enough, hungry enough to know more about who He was.

So He waited.

"Stay with us," they said. "It's nearly evening, and the day is almost over" (verse 29, CEB). It was hospitality to a stranger that became the game changer.

Jesus accepted their offer. Then He, the stranger, did something even stranger. Jesus, the guest, started acting like the host. When they sat at the table, Jesus took the bread and began giving thanks. This may mean nothing to us since we do not really have meal protocols. But in Jewish culture, the host always says the blessing. The guest never does. Yet here was this strange stranger talking as if the Scriptures were all about Him and acting as if the table and the meal were His to bless.

Luke recorded this action in a deliberate way, using the same set and sequence as the Passover—the last time Jesus took bread—and the feeding of the five thousand. Jesus "took the bread and blessed and broke it and gave it to them" (verse 30). And then the very next thing Luke tells us is that "their eyes were opened and they recognized him" (verse 31, CEB).

It's beautiful, isn't it? What made them realize it was Jesus was the way He *took bread, blessed it, broke it,* and *gave it* to them.

Of all the Jesus-like things to recognize Jesus by—the miracles, the teachings, the stories—it was the breaking of bread that opened their eyes.

Luke was making a point: There's something about bread that is *blessed, broken,* and *given* that makes us see Jesus. It shakes us out of our disillusionment and awakens us from our despair about religion. Once our eyes are lifted up, once they are opened to see Jesus, our hearts begin to burn within.

Yet it all began with an act of hospitality, with a guest acting like the host. And that's what we need to recover as a church if we're going to be given for the life of the world today.

Post-Christians

But first a bit more about our world. In many North American and European cities, there is another dynamic in this new kind of secular age. It's the sense of evolving beyond Christianity. Some people, particularly when they're referring to Europe, call this "post-Christian." It's a way of saying that the culture has moved beyond Christianity and yet can't define itself in terms other than in relation to what has been left behind. It cannot tell us what it is except to say what it is *not.* It is not Christian; it no longer believes Jesus is Lord or that the Cross had atoning power or that sin even exists.

And yet it clings to values, sensibilities, and impulses that are only present because of the influence of Christianity in its not-so-distant past. Christianity is vanishing, yet, to borrow Flannery O'Connor's vivid phrase, these cities remain "Christ-haunted."[4]

A few years ago I heard an award-winning author give a lecture on writing and the creative process. His presentation was inspiring, heartwarming, and hilarious. But what stood out to me were his comments about his own journey of faith. He kept describing himself as a "Catholic Buddhist" or a "Buddhist Catholic."

Never mind that each of those ancient religions would reject that sort of syncretism on the basic incompatibility of their competing claims. In twenty-first-century America, anything goes. One ought to be free to mix and match as we please, we think. The Catholic-Buddhist author kept talking about his work with references to themes like redemption, and I couldn't help but notice that redemption is not a theme he learned from Buddhism. The way he talked about darkness and light, good and evil, and hope and redemption demonstrated an unmistakably *Christian* use of these categories. Buddhism in its classic form does not make moral appraisals of good and evil. Those are equal and opposite parts of the same substance. Why should one be better than the other? Why should we hope for one to triumph over the other? But he couldn't shake it. The words Christianity gave him were still the way he worked out meaning in the world. He wanted to speak of redemption without naming the Redeemer.

That is a parable of our culture in the West. This is the generation that wants justice but not any sense of righteousness. We are hungry for community but have no taste for the Cross. We want the goods of the good news without the Christ of the gospel. We want the life of the kingdom without the claims of the King.

Maybe this is a reaction born of deep disappointment. Like the disciples on the road to Emmaus, our culture had hoped the church would be loving and kind, generous and gracious. What it found, all too often, was a church of angry actions engaged in a culture war. There are disillusioned post-Christians because *the church*—not Jesus—turned out to be different from what they hoped we would be. And instead of opening their eyes with our generous blessing, breaking, and giving of bread, we have made them look away in disgust because of our partisanship and reach for social and political power. Hearts are hardened—not burning and alive—because of our refusal to go into their homes and eat with them. We wanted nothing to do with these cultural enemies, and so they want nothing to do with us.

I know because our own church was caught up in the culture war. We cared about evangelism, but I suspect we loved power more. And when our founding senior pastor was himself caught in scandal in 2006, it only made the mocking cries from the city louder. In their eyes the hypocrisy couldn't have been clearer or the irony sharper. And while as Christians we do indeed believe in the redemption and cleansing of God's forgiveness—with God the story is never over—the damage in Colorado Springs had been done. "This is what all Christians are," people said. "Angry, hypocritical, liars. *This* is why we don't need religion. *This* is why Christians should not be allowed to have any form of social power, any currency of cultural influence."

"We had hoped . . ." they said. "But that's all over now. We're past that. Post-*that*."

It's hard to be given when the world wants nothing we're giving.

When All the Stars Are Gone

This sense of being closed off to religion is what Charles Taylor called the "immanent frame."[5] It's life without transcendence.

One of the ways to think about transcendence is as a source of meaning beyond this world. Something above and beyond, which informs and shapes the here and now, the visible and the tangible. Transcendence means we answer such questions as "How do we know what is good?" or "How do we know what is virtue?" or "How do we know what is morality?" We find the answers by pointing to some higher power or being or force—something beyond the frame of the world.

An "immanent frame," by contrast, is a way of filtering out the transcendent and framing around the immanent. It does not mean there is no God, just that it doesn't really matter if there is one. And even if God exists, the popular sentiment is that since we can't quite agree on what He's like or what He wants from us, we ought not bother at all. We can just bracket God out and enclose life in an immanent frame, in which all that *really* matters is that we love one another and live in harmony. That's hard enough as it is.

To change the metaphor of the immanent frame, consider the roof over the Wimbledon tennis court several years ago. If you're a tennis fan, you will know that Wimbledon is one of the most historic venues for tennis tournaments and the only one of the four major tournaments played on real grass. In 2006 the roof was removed,[6] and the arena had the open summer sky to match the fresh green grass. Lawn tennis, I guess, should feel like the outdoors. But a few years later, the decision was made to add a retractable roof to avoid rain delays and to allow matches to go on late into the night. When the roof was actually closed during an entire match in 2009, it had everyone's attention firmly fixed on the match. And it allowed the match to run more than an hour later than any previous match on Centre Court.[7] Here's the point: when a roof is closed over a sporting arena, it doesn't matter whether there are clouds or stars in the sky. All that matters is the match on the field.

This is the perfect metaphor for the secular age. We don't know whether there's *a* God or ten thousand gods or a force in the universe or even simply the Universe as a divine entity. We don't know. But what we do know is that there's a match taking place on the field of life that needs our attention. We've got to sort out our lives, and frankly, there are more pressing questions than who God is. We don't have time to deal with questions about religion, which have little to no bearing on how we actually live. And years of Christian hypocrisy in the public eye have only served to reinforce the suspicion that religion does not have any effect on how good a person's life is. So we close the roof to the heavens not because we've rejected God but because we don't have any use for Him.

Our challenge today in many parts of North America and Europe is not *militant atheism* but *indifferent agnosticism.* The person you meet at Starbucks is not likely going to say "I hate God, and I have ten reasons why!" But you might hear that man or woman say "I don't know, man, but what's the fuss about? Why is this such a big deal? Who cares? Can't we just love one another? Can't we just get along?"

When it comes to those goals, it seems Christians in particular have proved to be not only unhelpful but actually hurtful.

Christians have sometimes made their religion an impediment to the harmony and peace of a city. But if our *cultural hostility* was at least part of the problem, then maybe our *radical hospitality* may be part of the answer.

Luke told another story at the end of Acts that parallels the Emmaus Road account. Once again the action takes place outside religious spaces. In Luke's gospel the scene involves walking away from Jerusalem; in Acts it is an encounter on a ship bound for Rome. In Luke the turbulence is emotional and existential; in Acts there is an actual storm. In Luke we have disillusioned disciples; in Acts we have soldiers and criminals. In Luke the protagonist is Jesus; in Acts it is Paul, the apostle of Christ. In both there is bread that is blessed, broken, and given.

The buildup to that scene is momentous. Luke wrote that the storm had eclipsed the heavenly lights. "When neither sun nor stars appeared for many days, and no small tempest lay on us, all hope of our being saved was at last abandoned" (Acts 27:20).

This is where the metaphor of a "closed roof" takes on particular poignancy. When the heavens were closed off, the sailors could not navigate. Without the sun by day or the stars by night, how were they to know where they were? They had lost their bearings in the storm and had no means of regaining it.

What do you do when all the stars are gone? You make meaning where you can find it. A centurion on the ship took charge. Paul tried to speak to him, but he was ignored. The centurion, Luke explained, paid more attention to the captain and to the ship's owner than to some follower of a strange Messiah. This is an apt picture of the church in our age: we're trying to talk and gain the attention of a sinking world, but our voice is ignored while another—perhaps the voice of power and profits—is preferred. Christians are no longer anywhere near the cultural center.

Paul kept speaking, but not in an accusing way. He offered little rebuke and much hope. In fact, Paul's word to them when the heavens had been closed off and they had lost all hope was for them to "take heart" (verses 22, 25). The *worst thing,* as Frederick Buechner wrote, does not have to be the *last thing.* Things don't have to end in disaster. There *is* hope.

But the sailors wanted to take matters into their own hands. They wanted to be their own salvation. They tried to sneak off the ship onto a smaller boat. Paul warned them not to: "Unless these men stay in the ship, you cannot be saved" (verse 31). So the soldiers cut away the ropes to the boat, eliminating the option altogether.

This, too, is a metaphor for our human attempts in this secular age to make meaning for ourselves, to be fully alive by being true to ourselves. But we don't realize the futility in it. Is there a master more whimsical and cruel than we are to ourselves? And is there anything more tyrannical than the trends of the day? None of us gets to live without a yoke; everyone, as Bob Dylan sang, is "gonna have to serve somebody."[8] But only Jesus says, "Take my yoke upon you, and learn from me, for I am gentle and lowly in heart, and you will find rest for your souls. For my yoke is easy, and my burden is light" (Matthew 11:29–30).

In this dramatic closing narrative, Luke shows us that everyone is following *someone*—fisherman and Samaritans, sailors and soldiers. But only in following Jesus is there any hope of being saved.

Having awakened hope and exposed the lie, Paul then began to bear witness to the grace of God. The climactic moment of this story is when Paul, like Jesus at the close of Luke's gospel, "took bread, gave thanks to God in front of them all, then broke it and began to eat" (Acts 27:35, CEB).

There may be more that Luke, the consummate storyteller, wanted us to see. Only twice in both his gospel account and in the book of Acts combined did Luke use the Greek word *eucharisteo* (at the Passover scene in Luke 22 and here in Acts 27). The word means "thanksgiving," and it contains within it the word for grace or gift, *charis*. It is the giving of thanks for the gift of Jesus Christ; it is the thanksgiving over bread that makes us think of the Bread of Life.

In a hostile environment and in the midst of turbulence, Paul acted *eucharistically*. The bread on that ship was not what we might call "the Eucharist"—the Lord's Supper. But his taking of bread, giving thanks for it as a way of blessing it, and then breaking it and giving it to the sailors, soldiers, and prisoners on board was *eucharistic*.

It was a way of bearing witness to the grace of God in the middle of a terrible time. It was a way of saying that even here and even now—when all the stars are gone and when you can no longer see heaven—there is a God who is the source of all things, the giver of every good gift.

Like the Eucharist, this meal on a shipwreck was a meal of thanksgiving and a meal of hope. And it was an act of *radical hospitality.*

RADICAL HOSPITALITY

When our new senior pastor, Brady Boyd, arrived in August 2007, he helped us realize something that should have been obvious to us: our posture needed to change. We were a church that had been broken by scandal. And we were about to be a church shaken by tragedy—a shooting occurred on our church campus after a Sunday service in December 2007. Two teenage girls lost their lives.

We didn't need to escape our brokenness. We needed to discover how our givenness could flow out of it. We needed to trade in our megaphones and manifestos for towels and tables.

Jesus, on the night of the Passover meal with His disciples, got up from the table, took off his outer garment, and grabbed a towel. If Jesus took a towel and began to wash the dirty feet of His betrayer and denier, then surely the body of Christ ought not take a posture of superiority and yell at the world.

If the church is Christ's availability in the world, then our presence in our communities needs to be shaped by the way *Christ* would inhabit those spaces. N. T. Wright fires our imagination about just what it might look like for the church to live out a Christ-shaped calling in the world:

> The Christian vocation is to be in prayer, in the Spirit, at
> the place where the world is in pain, and as we embrace that
> vocation, we discover it to be the way of following Christ,
> shaped according to his messianic vocation to the cross,
> with arms outstretched, holding on simultaneously to the
> pain of the world and to the love of God. . . . Learn new

ways of praying with and from the pain, the brokenness, of that crucial part of the world where God has placed you.[9]

This was exactly what we began to do at New Life Church. Pastor Brady and a team began meeting ministries and agencies in our city to discover the places of pain and to identify gaps in the existing systems and organizations. They discovered that there was nowhere for women between the ages of eighteen and sixty-five who were uninsured or underinsured to get quality health care. So they began the journey of launching the Dream Centers of Colorado Springs Women's Clinic. As of this writing, the clinic has had over eight thousand appointments covering everything from checkups to prenatal care. It is the only clinic in the area that offers free medical, behavioral health, and other wraparound services. Taking a holistic approach, the clinic is a place where women can find not only medical care but also spiritual and social services.

Along the way we learned that another glaring gap of care in our city was a safe place for homeless single moms and their kids to stay. Many of these women are fleeing situations of abuse or harmful environments for them and their kids. So with the help of generous donors, we were able to buy and remodel a small apartment complex we call Mary's Home. It is a safe place where women can heal, develop skills, and gain access to college classes. It is designed to help women begin to break the cycle of poverty over a five-year span.

This is a long way from engaging in culture wars. We are a church who walks with a limp. We have wrestled with God in the dead of night and had to confess our sins by name. Like Jacob the

Deceiver, we were Evangelicals the Power Hungry. But God returned to us our true name. He restored our vocation to be carriers of the blessing, to embrace our brokenness, and to step into a new kind of givenness.

In an age when belief is contested, when religion is a private matter with little bearing on real life, the church needs to recover the art of radical hospitality. But this is a kind of hospitality that is more than making our sacred spaces ready for others; it is a kind of hospitality that we exhibit by showing up in someone else's space with a posture of openness. Think about it: How many times do church leaders show up at gatherings that we have not convened? How often do we as Christians want people to come with us to church, while we exit the places where the rest of the community is? We want people to come to us, but are we willing to go to them?

Luke's stories describe Jesus and Paul showing up in nonreligious places, meeting people where they are in the journey, whether they are disillusioned or even ideologically hostile. We need to listen and learn and then enter into the places of pain in our communities. Like Jesus coming alongside the disillusioned disciples, we need to walk gently into the spaces where the unchurched and post-Christians have gone. Like Paul standing up in the middle of a storm to speak to terrified soldiers and sailors and prisoners, we need to go into the heart of the tempest as a way of saying that even there Christ is present. Sometimes it means retelling the story of Scripture in a more beautiful and Christ-centered way, the way Jesus did; sometimes, like Paul, we simply stand up and testify to grace.

When we find the disillusioned disciples walking away with downcast eyes, when we find skeptical unbelievers trying to survive a shipwreck, our calling is to offer radical hospitality. Like Jesus acting as host of a meal that was not His, like Paul on a ship that was not under his command, we can find a way to reach out to those in the world and stand in the midst of their questions and pain, their disappointments and fear. We can take bread, bless it, break it, and give it to them.

We ourselves can become the bread that is blessed, broken, and given for them, for their lives—yes, even for the life of the world.

Postlude

The King's Feast

"What are you hungry for?" This is quite possibly the worst question to ask children on a road trip. You will either get the silence of indecision or the torrent of conflicting opinions.

One child will blurt out, "I want Burger Palace!"

"No, I *hate* Burger Palace," another child will say, overstating her opinion just to spite the sibling who suggested it, probably because of a spat they had just had.

"Well, what do *you* want then?"

"Burrito World! I like their rice and chicken."

"You always want rice and chicken. That is *so* boring."

The conversation will then devolve into a series of accusations about what the other "always" does. Or about how one child is *so* picky or boring or bossy. Before long the inquiry into food turns into a discourse on each other's idiosyncratic dietary habits.

Once in a while, though, on the long drive through Nowhere, a sign will pop up for a restaurant, and everyone will be in one accord: "Yes! Chick-fil-A! Let's stop there!" And just like that, the "What are you hungry for?" dilemma is resolved.

Humans are hungry creatures. We were created with appetites. The first need we were aware of as newborns was the need for food. We took a breath and then cried for milk. Life begins with eating.

But as it turns out, death comes by eating wrongly.

So it was in the Garden of Eden. Adam and Eve were surrounded by delights when God spoke to them about food. It's interesting that the first recorded conversation between God and the crown of His creation is about *what to eat* (Genesis 2). It's also important to note that Adam and Eve had appetites and a need to eat before the Fall. Hunger is not a result of sin but rather part of the way God created us.

Hunger becomes a metaphor for all our appetites, and food becomes a picture of our source of sustenance—the things we cannot go without. What we choose to eat reveals what we have built our lives to need. So when the opening story in the Bible shows God setting humans in the world and directing their appetites, it is trying to tell us something. The whole trajectory of life and death is determined by where we direct our appetites. If we begin to hunger most deeply for things that cannot satisfy fully, we are on our way to death. But if we feast on that which fills, we will truly live.

As the story of God and His people continues, we find the children of Israel in the wilderness, hungry. God's provision of manna from heaven is a picture of how the people of God are meant to rely on God as their source and supplier. The song of the psalmist beckoning us to "taste and see that the LORD is good" (Psalm 34:8) calls us away from feeding on that which will not ultimately sustain us. Other psalms compare the steadfast love of the Lord to a rich feast that always satisfies our desires (see 36:8).

When it's all said and done, the scene in Revelation meant to evoke hope is a great wedding feast, and among the final words of the entire apocalyptic vision is the injunction to come and drink (see Revelation 22:17).

Food and drink are the most basic human needs. And they are a picture for us of our humanness. We were not made to be self-sufficient. We need something from the outside to sustain us, to nourish us, to feed us. Ultimately, we need the Creator Himself. In Deuteronomy God reminded the people of Israel who had journeyed out of the wilderness and into a land where they could raise their own food that they should not "live on bread alone but on every word that comes from the mouth of the LORD" (Deuteronomy 8:3, CSB).

We were created as hungry creatures so that we would never forget our Creator. We can direct our hunger toward that which will not truly satisfy, but doing so will eventually lead to spiritual malnourishment and death. Better to train ourselves to desire the Bread of Life and Living Water. Only then shall we truly live.

FORMED BY A FEAST

When people find out I'm from Malaysia, and they have visited there, it doesn't take long before they exclaim, "Oh, the food!" This is because Malaysia is known for its cuisine. It is a veritable curry pot of Southeast Asian flavors, mixing the spices and sauces of India, China, Thailand, Malaya, and more.

I remember coming from school and going right to the kitchen, where my mother would be chopping onions and garlic, beginning the long and loving preparation of our family dinner. She would hand me some spices and point me toward the mortar and pestle, where I would do my best to grind them up without inadvertently squirting bits into my eye. Then as the spices I had been working on attained the right texture, they were added to the meat. When the garlic and onions hit the hot oil in the pan, an aroma filled the kitchen that made me almost taste the meal to come.

I have come to understand that not everyone views food the way Malaysians do. For some, a meal is a necessary evil, an interruption to the other things one most do in a day or a troublesome recurring task that requires an inordinate amount of work just to keep people happy. Food, for many people, is met with quiet and stoic gratitude. One merely nods to acknowledge the beginning of mealtime, then dutifully moves the spoon from the bowl of goulash or stroganoff or stew to one's mouth until it is gone. Then it's time for chores to resume.

But this is not how my family did meals. Meals were loud. Not because there were so many of us, since there were usually only four of us around the table (my parents, my sister, and me). It wasn't the number of people that accounted for the volume; it was the way we responded to food.

"Oh, this smells soooo good!" and "My goodness! This looks amazing!" The anticipatory praise would then be followed by urges from my parents to take as much as we wanted. There was much more in the kitchen. We had not even taken a bite but were already thinking about seconds. To be clear, we were not gluttons; we did not indulge at every meal. But dinners were delights to be savored, not duties to be done. Thus, as with other delights, a dinner is to be praised by the recipient and to be doled out generously by the host.

I'll never forget when my wife first experienced the overpowering hospitality of my family. We were in Malaysia on a visit—a very special visit. It was on this trip that I proposed to Holly. On one of the evenings after our engagement, we had gone out to eat with my parents and my aunty and uncle from Sri Lanka. Holly, uneasy about all the curries and sauces, served herself a small portion. Only a few years before this evening, my wife had never eaten Mexican food or Chinese food or even *rice.*

My Aunty Yvonne, who, as you may recall, is my mother's eldest sister, was eager to play the generous hostess and promptly offered Holly more food. Holly smiled and declined.

"Come, come, have some more," Aunty Yvonne insisted.

"No, no, really, it's okay. I'm good," Holly sweetly said again.

"Come," my aunty said with a kind but stronger tone. "Eat!"

And with that, she piled Holly's plate with more curry. How could anyone possibly not want more? Life may be more than food, but for Malaysians *life happens at a table.*

The truth is, life *always* happens at a table. We are feeding on something, feasting somewhere. The only question is whether it will bring us life or lead us to death.

Two Banquets

There are two tables set before us. God has prepared a Table for us with His own body and blood as our bread and cup. And the world sets a table before us, offering its delights.

Nowhere in the Gospels is the contrast between the banquets—the kingdom of God and the kingdoms of the world—
more stark than in Mark's gospel. Both Matthew and Mark set the
story of John the Baptist's beheading right before the story of Jesus
feeding the five thousand. But Mark makes the arrangement feel
even more intentional by telling us that Herod "prepared a feast"
(Mark 6:21, CEB). That phrase struck me. "A feast." Well, wouldn't
you say that Jesus feeding five thousand people is also a feast?

Looking at the two feasts side by side, one can't help but notice
the differences between the two kings and the kingdoms they represent. For one, the people at the feasts were vastly different. Herod
prepared a feast for "his high-ranking officials and military officers
and Galilee's leading residents" (verse 21, CEB). This was a party for
the power players, for the "who's who," the movers and shakers.
But Jesus found a crowd who had invited themselves. These were
people from various cities in the area who arrived at the spot where
they anticipated Jesus and His disciples would be. These people
must have been desperate for something.

Herod was in control of the guest list and made sure there
were only guests who could give him something. Jesus found an
uninvited crowd who wanted something from Him.

Yet Jesus looked at the crowd and "had compassion on them"
(verse 34, CEB). We don't know what Herod thought about his
guests. But we do know that a girl's dancing pleased him and got
him in a request-granting mood. He told her to ask for whatever she
wished, up to half his kingdom (see verse 23). Jesus taught the
crowd "many things" (verse 34, CEB). And then He fed them.

At Herod's feast *performance* was everything—please the king and you just might get what you *want*. At Jesus's feast *compassion* was everything. Because the King is already full of love for you, He gives you what you *need*. The people never asked for something to eat; Jesus knew that they were hungry. They didn't have to perform for Him to notice them. He *saw* them from the beginning. And He loved them. So He fed them—with His words and with bread.

The climactic moment of Herod's feast was someone's death—not just a death, but a murder. The execution of John the Baptist was the *real* story of Herod's birthday party. The conclusion of Jesus's feast was abundance. There were twelve baskets filled with bread and fish, and everyone there had already eaten till they were full.

At Herod's party there was never enough—never enough power or pleasure or control. Someone had to lose for someone else to win. Someone had to die for others to live. And even though it may not have been Herod's desire to behead John, it served him just fine—the troublemaker would be silenced. One can never be too suspicious about potential revolutionaries. But at Jesus's banquet there was *more than enough*. There was enough for everyone to be filled, and then some more. Moreover, while Herod's commands created chaos—imagine a party where someone's head is brought in on a platter!—Jesus's commands brought order. He told the disciples how to organize the crowd so they could be fed.

Herod's feast will always end in death. Jesus's feast will always lead to abundance.

At the two feasts there are two different ways of becoming a guest, two different ways of making a request or getting a need met. And there are two different ways for the story to end.

The first story is about power, performance, and ultimately death. The second story is about desperation, hunger, and ultimately life.

Feast with Herod and you may feel powerful, but you will be bound to perform. In the end you will be left with chaos and death.

Feast with Jesus and you can come desperate and needy, tired and hungry, and you will be fed and nourished. In the end you will be given an abundance of life.

But this is not just a story about two feasts; this is about two kings and two kingdoms.

Mark tells us that when Jesus saw the crowd, He had compassion on them for "they were like sheep without a shepherd" (verse 34, CEB).

This is significant, not just a throwaway line. The shepherd imagery in the Bible is not some sort of therapeutic image of care and nurture. A shepherd was the most comprehensive metaphor an agrarian society could come up with: it represented a protector, physician, provider, and guide.

So it makes sense that when the prophets and poets of Israel wrote about their king, they referred to him as a *shepherd*. One prophet, Ezekiel, had a particularly scathing review—offered on behalf of God—of the kings of Israel. He called them the shepherds of Israel but then accused them of having only "tended themselves" (Ezekiel 34:2, CEB). Instead of tending the sheep, they drank the milk, wore the wool, and slaughtered "the fat animals" (verse 3, CEB). They didn't "strengthen the weak, heal the sick, bind up the injured, bring back the strays, or seek out the lost." Instead, they used "force to rule them with injustice" (verse 4, CEB). In short, the shepherds of Israel had not lived up to the metaphor; they were not protectors, physicians, providers, or guides. They failed at the job description for a good king.

The very next verse of Ezekiel's divine tirade includes the lines that Mark would quote: "Without a shepherd, my flock was scattered; and when it was scattered, it became food for all the wild animals" (verse 5, CEB).

Then the Lord declared through Ezekiel that He is "against the shepherds" (verse 10, CEB). And not only that, He will come to do the job Himself.

The LORD God proclaims: I myself will search for my flock and seek them out. As a shepherd seeks out the flock when some in the flock have been scattered, so will I seek out my flock. I will rescue them from all the places where they were scattered during the time of clouds and thick darkness. I will gather and lead them out from the countries and peoples, and I will bring them to their own fertile land. I will feed them on Israel's highlands, along the riverbeds, and in all the inhabited places. I will feed them in good pasture, and their sheepfold will be there, on Israel's lofty highlands. On Israel's highlands, they will lie down in a secure fold and feed on green pastures. I myself will feed my flock and make them lie down. This is what the LORD God says. I will seek out the lost, bring back the

strays, bind up the wounded, and strengthen the weak.
But the fat and the strong I will destroy, because I will
tend my sheep with justice. (verses 11–16, CEB)

Now we see it: the feeding of the five thousand is not a random story of Jesus doing some sort of party trick. It was a sign that the kingdom of God was arriving and that Jesus Himself was the true King.[1] Herod was not the real king, and his banquet was not the real feast. Jesus is the king who provides a bounty for the people.

So where are you feasting? Are you at Herod's banquet, hoping to satisfy yourself on the kind of power and pleasure the world can offer? Are you chasing influence and significance the world's way, by working harder or trying to get in with the right group? Are you obsessively posting on social media, trying to get your "likes" and "views" up, hoping to be seen? That feast won't fill you. It will lead only to death. Or are you desperately following Jesus, clinging to every word, hungry and needy? Are you opening the Scriptures, sitting and listening, shaping your life by His cross-shaped love? It will be for your good, bringing you nourishment, healing, and health.

The table you choose reveals the king you serve.

THE GREAT INVITATION

The approach to Jesus's table begins with good news and a great invitation. In the traditional version of the Anglican liturgy, there are a series of Scriptures pronounced to prepare the hearts of the people for communion. Four lines from the New Testament are crafted together to compose what is known as "the Comfortable Words."

Remember, in medieval church services prior to the Reformation, there was no public moment when people confessed their sins together and received absolution together. One had to go individually to the priest to do that. And only *after* doing that could you receive communion. Since the Reformers wanted people to be able to receive communion weekly—just as early Christians had done for centuries when the church began—they needed a weekly corporate opportunity to confess their sins and to hear that God had forgiven them.

But how could they trust this was true? What if this was all too good to be true? These people did not have Bibles in their homes. They could not search the Scriptures for themselves. They needed something built into that moment in the service to comfort them. And so Thomas Cranmer, the English Reformer, inserted these "Comfortable Words" there, right after they had confessed their sins and heard forgiveness announced again. He wanted them to know God in Christ was already calling to them, had already loved them in their unlovely state, and had made provision for their forgiveness.

The first "word" is a quote from Matthew's gospel. It is Jesus speaking: "Come to me, all you that are weary and are carrying heavy burdens, and I will give you rest" (Matthew 11:28, NRSV).

This verse was Cranmer's unique addition. It's a powerful choice of an opening. It speaks to our weariness; it shows us that God is not so high above us that He does not have compassion on our state. The sequence opens with an *invitation*—"Come to me!" Don't go to cracked and dry cisterns (see Jeremiah 2:13). Don't run after false gods. Don't go to shepherds who are not true shepherds.

Don't look for provision, protection, healing, and guidance from people or things that cannot give what you are looking for. Don't ask of someone or something that which it cannot give. Do not, as Isaiah said, spend your money on "that which is not bread, and your labor for that which does not satisfy" (Isaiah 55:2).

Don't do that. Not because God is fussy and full of arbitrary rules. But because God knows He has made us for Himself and that "our hearts are restless till they find rest" in Him.[2]

The second "word" is from John's gospel: "For God so loved the world that he gave his only Son, so that everyone who believes in him may not perish but may have eternal life" (John 3:16, NRSV).

The focus pivots now from *human weariness* to *divine longing*. It is not just we who need God; it is God who *loves* us. The God who has no need is in His very being love—the triune God has His being in communion. And this love overflows. In fact, the historian George Marsden wrote that the great American preacher Jonathan Edwards saw the "universe [as] an explosion of God's glory. Perfect goodness, beauty, and love radiate from God and draw creatures to ever increasingly share in the Godhead's joy and delight."[3]

The same God whose glory and love erupted into the creation of the cosmos made a way to redeem this world that He loves. The truest thing about the world is that it is loved by God. The truest thing about you is that you are loved by God. How do we know? Because as Jesus invites us to come to Him, we see that God Himself sent His Son to *us*.

The third "word" is from Paul's letter to Timothy and is a

summary of the gospel: "The saying is sure and worthy of full acceptance, that Christ Jesus came into the world to save sinners" (1 Timothy 1:15, NRSV).

This is the first mention of sin. Only after naming our human weariness and the divine longing, only after grounding us in God's love, do the Comfortable Words speak to us about sin. Yes, there is a great barrier between us and God; there is an impediment to our coming to Him. It is our sin. So God came to us to do for us what we could never do for ourselves.

The fourth and final "word" is from one of John's letters and carries a deeply pastoral exhortation: "But if anyone does sin, we have an advocate with the Father, Jesus Christ the righteous; and he is the atoning sacrifice for our sins, and not for ours only but also for the sins of the whole world" (1 John 2:1–2, NRSV).

Here is the word of hope: Jesus is our advocate. This is courtroom language. We might have expected that. But we thought maybe there would be a verse that reminds us of God as a judge. In medieval art throughout England, there was often a large mural on the church wall above the altar of an imagined scene of Judgment Day. Holly and I saw one in a church in Stratford-upon-Avon a few years ago. But the painting had been scrubbed off, or whitewashed, like so many other medieval paintings. Some people say this was because the Reformers hated art. In some cases that may have been true. But other times it was because they didn't want people coming to worship with an image of judgment before them. Cranmer wanted Christians to see Jesus as their advocate.

Take the whole sequence of the Comfortable Words together and you begin to see a marvelous picture of God:[4]

Jesus *calls us to Himself.*

Jesus *was sent because God loves us.*

Jesus *came to save us.*

Jesus *is for us.*

TAKEN

No wonder Cranmer wanted people to next hear, "Lift up your hearts!" After hearing all the words before that, we can only respond, "We lift them up to the Lord!"

And the leader, anticipating the eruption of praise building in us, says, "Let us give thanks to the Lord our God!" Maybe with additional emphasis on "our"!

And we say, "It is right to give Him thanks and praise!"

How could we not?

When we glimpse this Jesus, when we grasp this good news, our hearts are taken by the love of God.

The word *taken*—thanks in no small part to Liam Neeson and a series of movies—might conjure up frightening or violent images. *Taken* seems to refer to something done against someone's will.

But to see ourselves as bread means to willingly surrender, to allow the Lord to *take* us. We lift up our hearts to the Lord and allow ourselves to be *taken* by Him. We sometimes speak of people in love as being *taken* with one another.

This was at the heart of what Cranmer was up to in putting

together the worship service for the Church of England. He believed deeply that "divine gracious love . . . inspires grateful human love."[5]

Taken by the love of God, we allow ourselves to be *blessed, broken,* and *given* for the glory of God and for the life of the world.

TOMORROW

Lord willing, tomorrow morning I will hear the worship song that is my morning alarm play at 6:15. I'll roll over, fumble on the bed-side table for my phone, and hit the snooze button like an oaf swatting a fly. Ten minutes after that, it will sound again, and I'll finally get up and begin getting ready for the day. At some point in the process—moments after becoming conscious—I will turn my heart to the Lord. I might say, very simply, "Good morning, Holy Spirit" or "Thank You, Jesus, for this day."

After getting ready for the day, I'll likely find our younger two children awake—wildly so. Odds are they will be wrestling on our bed or chasing each other over a toy. I will look wistfully at the chair that sits by our bedroom window, imagining a more serene setting for reading the Bible. Alas, this will have to do. I will gently ask our children to play somewhere else while I pray and read. As I sit in the chair, I will close my eyes and breathe in deeply, repeating again a prayer of thankfulness to Jesus. Then I'll reach for the red prayer book with the whole book of Psalms in the back, complete with a prayer to pray after each psalm. If it's a good morning, I'll read two or three psalms and slow down to pray the prayers. If it's a typical morning, I'll read one and try to pray it meaningfully.

After reading a passage from Scripture—a book of the Bible I'm reading through or a collection of texts from the daily reading guide I'm using—the din of children's voices will get louder. Holly will remind me that we're running out of time before we have to leave the house. I'll run downstairs to help with breakfast. One or two children will change their minds about how they want their eggs—"Scrambled!" "No, fried!" The number of pieces of toast will change; oatmeal will get spilled; we'll be all out of milk after the cereal has been poured. Then someone will look at the clock and blurt out with all the alarm of the Mad Hatter, "We're late!"

Usually that someone is me. We'll go bounding out the door, stumbling into two cars headed in two different directions. Or if it's a homeschooling day, the kids will stay while I leave—and my wife will be left trying to corral the children to start their work or do their chores or both.

Yet, in that blur, there are smiles and hugs and prayers and kisses. Little expressions of affection and affirmation—"I love you" and "Have a great day"—remind us of the blessing. We are God's, and we are loved. There is a great story with a beginning and an ending in which we get to play a part.

At work I will spend time answering emails, sitting in staff meetings that can feel light or heavy on any given week, and meeting with people—usually congregants—over lunch and coffee. At various points throughout the day, I will be struck by the beauty and the sorrow of it all. Life—this glorious, turbulent, unexpected ride—is unbearably glorious, even if its glory is hidden in the ordinary and messy moments.

On the way home odds are pretty good that with four kids in dance or soccer or music, I'll pick someone up from an activity and maybe even drive other kids in our carpool. At home, when I walk in the door, our younger two will—hopefully still—run to greet me. I'll be tempted to keep checking my phone, but their eager smiles will coax me to set it down somewhere and ignore it, at least for an hour or two.

During dinner prep with Holly and our older two children, we'll catch up on the day. She will ask, "How was your day? Who'd you meet with today?" I'll go through the list of appointments somewhat mechanically, knowing that it won't satisfy the counselor in her. But by this point, I'm *spent*. Not drained; spent. I've given out or been given out for the sake of others.

Besides, how would I recapture it all? How could I describe weeping with the older man over lunch or the kicked-in-the-gut feeling after hearing about a parent's fight for her child's health? How could I give a play-by-play of the conversation over coffee with a young person grappling with doubt and a deconstructing faith? How do I explain how a business person is allowing her vocation to be part of God's kingdom mission, using her gifts and expertise to lead to the flourishing of others?

Yet I will try. Because the beauty of what I get to do is be a witness: witness to a story becoming *blessed* as God returns people to their origins and restores their identity; witness to a story that may have been *broken* by failure or frailty or the fallenness of the world but is now being opened up to the grace of God; witness to a story that is now bringing blessing to others, that is being *given* for the sake of someone else in our church or in our community.

Some days, I get to see it, to really see it. But even when I don't, I still believe it. This is what Jesus does with our lives when we place them in His hands. He takes our stories and makes them sacred; He makes them something more.

Your tomorrow may be different from mine. You may live alone or with roommates. You may hate your job or not have one. You may find it hard to see anything beautiful or worthwhile in the moments of your day. You may feel like you're not a witness to much except the depravity of the world. Your own story may just seem too plain or too messed up or too incoherent. You may wonder, *Is there even a story?*

And yet, there is Jesus, ready to take what you place in His hands. It is these very moments and your very story that He wants to bless and break and give.

So come. Place your life, your whole story, in the hands of Jesus. Offer it to Him now. Pray with me,

Jesus, I am Yours.

Bless me. Break me. Give me.

Take my story and make it sacred; make it more than what it could be without You.

Make me blessed, broken, and given.

Acknowledgments

This was a practice before it ever appeared on a page. It was our manifesto before it was a manuscript. We began using this language—blessed, broken, given—when we began New Life Downtown as a congregation in 2012. But the truth is, the seeds of this have been at work in New Life Church for years, said and expressed in various ways. So to the people of New Life Church, thank you for always being a church that looks for God at work even in the ordinary, for learning to walk through pain together with humility and vulnerability, and for living with the conviction that the reason we exist is not for ourselves. Thank you for embracing the practice of coming to the Table, and for making Table language a metaphor for our worship, our life together, and our mission as a church. You have shown me how beautiful the gospel really is.

I have a deep and special gratitude for our congregation, New Life Downtown, for showing me what this looks like each week. Thank you for letting me be a witness to God's grace at work in you and for trusting me to share your stories. You are the "living epistle"; you are this book in living community. I—and this book—have been formed by our life and worship together.

To Pastor Brady for encouraging my exploration and for giving me a place to practice embodying it. Your humility, wisdom, and friendship have been a well of life to me.

To Patton Dodd for slipping me a book by Schmemann years ago and, in doing so, opening the portal further into a sacramental way of seeing.

To my wife, Holly, for all the big and small ways you remind me of my blessedness, love me in my brokenness, and lead me in my givenness. You shape our family and our home in ways that embody these words. Your support and sacrifice and vision and intentionality are gifts that make me deeply grateful to walk with you. And to our children for living this together with us. In our ordinariness and our messiness, we are blessed, we are broken, and we are given. You show me what this looks like every day, and I am better for it.

To my parents and my sister for making life happen at a table—delicious food and vigorous conversations have always been the norm, and I'm grateful to have been formed by both.

To my faithful friends and brothers for the way we've prayed over and wept with one another, laughed together, and walked together as we've pushed one another to maturity; for reading and thinking out loud together; and for listening and laughing and encouraging me along the lonely road of writing.

To my agent, Don Jacobson, for being patient with writing this proposal and for prodding and poking and sometimes provoking until the word that was "like fire shut up in my bones" came out onto the page.

To my editor, Andrew Stoddard, for believing in this project, for championing it along the way, and for bringing not only your writing instincts but also your theological and historical acumen to each page. Your expertise made this book more compelling, and your friendship made the process a joy.

To the team at Multnomah for being enthusiastic and attentive throughout the process of creating this and for being proactive and creative in dreaming up how to share it with the world.

These pages contain a life message that has been formed by the people in my life. The ones I've mentioned are meant to represent countless more.

Finally, to you the reader for being intrigued enough to pick up this book. My deepest prayer is for these pages to be not a transfer of information but a firing of your imagination. As it was for the disciples on the road to Emmaus when Christ took bread, blessed it, broke it, and gave it for them, I pray that the Holy Spirit will reveal Christ to you in these pages and that your own heart may burn within.

Notes

Chapter 1: Glorious Bread

1. Mark Woods, "What God Does When We Pray: How Quantum Theory Helps Us Understand Intercession," *Christian Today,* October 18, 2015, www.christiantoday .com/article/what-god-does-when-we-pray-how-quantum -theory-helps-us-understand-intercession/67710.htm.

2. Stanley J. Grenz, *Theology for the Community of God* (Grand Rapids, MI: Eerdmans, 2000), 513.

3. Gerard Manley Hopkins, "God's Grandeur," *Poems and Prose* (1953; repr., London: Penguin Classics, 1985), 27.

4. Wikipedia, s.v., "Veni Creator Spiritus," last updated January 1, 2019, 14:52, https://en.wikipedia.org/wiki /Veni_Creator_Spiritus.

Chapter 2: Origins

1. E. C. Lucas, "Cosmology," in *Dictionary of the Old Testament: Pentateuch,* ed. T. Desmond Alexander and David W. Baker (Downers Grove, IL: InterVarsity, 2003), 132.

2. Joshua J. Mark, "Enuma Elish: The Babylonian Epic of Creation—Full Text," Ancient History Encyclopedia, www .ancient.eu/article/225/enuma-elish---the-babylonian-epic -of-creation---fu/.

3. Lucas, "Cosmology," 132.

4. "HaMotzi: The Blessing over Bread," Hebrew for Christians, www.hebrew4christians.com/Blessings/Daily_Blessings /Food_Blessings/Over_Bread/over_bread.html.

5. Alexander Schmemann, *For the Life of the World: Sacraments and Orthodoxy,* 2nd ed. (Crestwood, NY: St. Vladimir's Seminary Press, 1973), 14.

6. Stanley J. Grenz, *Theology for the Community of God* (Grand Rapids, MI: Eerdmans, 2000), 513.

Chapter 3: Names

1. Bill Bryson, *Made in America: An Informal History of American English* (London: Black Swan, 2016), 115.

2. Bryson, *Made in America,* 116.

3. Bryson, *Made in America,* 117.

4. Alan Kreider, *The Patient Ferment of the Early Church: The Improbable Rise of Christianity in the Roman Empire* (Grand Rapids, MI: Baker Academic, 2016), 38.

5. Phil Knight, *Shoe Dog: A Memoir by the Creator of Nike* (New York: Simon & Schuster, 2016), 191–92.

6. Alexander Schmemann, *For the Life of the World: Sacraments and Orthodoxy,* 2nd ed. (Crestwood, NY: St. Vladimir's Seminary Press, 1973), 15.

7. Schmemann, *For the Life of the World,* 15.

Chapter 4: Tables

1. N. T. Wright, *The Day the Revolution Began: Reconsidering the Meaning of Jesus's Crucifixion* (San Francisco: HarperOne, 2016), 291.

2. Robert W. Jenson, *A Theology in Outline: Can These Bones Live?* (New York: Oxford University Press, 2016), 97.

Chapter 5: Shadows and Shame

1. This terminology comes from Carl Jung and has influenced many paradigms of counseling even in the Christian context. See, for example, Howard Clinebell, *Basic Types of Pastoral Care and Counseling: Resources for the Ministry of Healing and Growth* (Nashville: Abingdon, 2011).

2. Jack McCallum, *Dream Team: How Michael, Magic, Larry, Charles, and the Greatest Team of All Time Conquered the World and Changed the Game of Basketball Forever* (New York: Ballantine, 2013), 188.

3. McCallum, *Dream Team,* 189.

4. Leonard Cohen, "Anthem" *The Future,* copyright © 1992, Columbia Records.

5. Andrew Curry, "World's Oldest Temple to Be Restored," *National Geographic,* National Geographic Society, January 20, 2016, news.nationalgeographic.com/2016/01 /150120-gobekli-tepe-oldest-monument-turkey-archaeology/.

6. Randall Collins, *Interaction Ritual Chains* (Princeton, NJ: Princeton University Press, 2004), 111.

7. Bill Arnold, an esteemed Old Testament professor at Asbury Theological Seminary in Wilmore, Kentucky, wrote that based on everything we know about religion in the ancient world, Israel in the Old Testament was the only nation that had a sacrifice that specifically addressed guilt. Bill T. Arnold, "Was Ancient Israel Just Like Its Neighbors? A

Singular Israel in a Pluralistic World," Seedbed, June 30, 2016, www.seedbed.com/was-ancient-israel-just-like-its-neighbors-a-singular-israel-in-a-pluralistic-world/.

8. Blake Gopnik, "Golden Seams: The Japanese Art of Mending Ceramics," *The Washington Post,* March 3, 2009, www.washingtonpost.com/wp-dyn/content/article/2009/03/02/AR2009030202723.html.

9. Gopnik, "Golden Seams."

Chapter 6: Suffering and Pain

1. It's important to note here that mental health issues often cannot be addressed through prayer alone. Enlisting the help of counselors, taking medication, and even changing diet and exercise may be part of the journey. Do not hear me say that spiritual answers are all we need. God works through all of it.

2. "St. Teresa of Avila Quotes," *Carmel, Garden of God* (blog), August 26, 2012, https://carmelourladysdovecote.wordpress.com/2012/08/26/st-teresa-of-avila-quotes/.

3. St. Augustine, "Enchiridion on Faith, Hope and Love," Catholic Treasury, www.catholictreasury.info/books/enchiridion/ench8.php.

4. Wikipedia, s.v. "Felix culpa," last modified November 21, 2018, 05:00, https://en.wikipedia.org/wiki/Felix_culpa.

Chapter 7: Confession and Community

1. You see this in Psalm 51:18, which pleads for God's help in rebuilding the walls of Jerusalem, a reference to the ruin they returned to after exile, long after David's reign.

2. Sally Lloyd-Jones, *The Jesus Storybook Bible: Every Story Whispers His Name* (Grand Rapids, MI: ZonderKidz, 2007), 36, 74, 134, 173, 200, 227, 270, 331.

3. Richard Dawkins, *The God Delusion* (Boston: Houghton Mifflin Harcourt, 2008), 51.

4. *Parks and Recreation*, season 2, episode 16, "Galentine's Day," directed by Ken Kwapis, written by Michael Schur, aired February 11, 2010, on NBC.

5. Eric Westervelt, "Stumbling upon Miniature Memorials to Nazi Victims," NPR, May 31, 2012, www.npr.org/2012/05/31/153943491/stumbling-upon-miniature-memorials-to-nazi-victims.

6. Elie Wiesel, "A God Who Remembers," NPR, April 7, 2008, www.npr.org/2008/04/07/89357808/a-god-who-remembers.

7. See Fleming Rutledge's excellent treatment of these themes in *The Crucifixion: Understanding the Death of Jesus Christ* (Grand Rapids, MI: Eerdmans, 2015), especially page 132.

Chapter 9: For One Another

1. Robert Louis Wilken, *The Christians as the Romans Saw Them* (New Haven, CT: Yale University Press, 2003), 58.

2. Alan Kreider, *The Patient Ferment of the Early Church: The Improbable Rise of Christianity in the Roman Empire* (Grand Rapids, MI: Baker Academic, 2016), 65–68.

3. Kreider, *Patient Ferment*, 66.

4. Gary B. Ferngren, *Medicine and Health Care in Early Christianity* (Baltimore: Johns Hopkins University Press, 2009), 114, quoted in Kreider, *Patient Ferment*, 67.

5. Kreider, *Patient Ferment,* 67–68.

6. Rodney Stark, *The Rise of Christianity: How the Obscure, Marginal Jesus Movement Became the Dominant Religious Force in the Western World in a Few Centuries* (Princeton, NJ: Princeton University Press, 1996), 89–91.

7. To use Nietzsche's phrase made popular in Christian circles by Eugene Peterson.

8. This is the premise of Kreider's *Patient Ferment.*

9. N. T. Wright, *The Challenge of Jesus: Rediscovering Who Jesus Was and Is* (Downers Grove, IL: InterVarsity, 1999), 68.

10. Wright, 69.

11. John M. G. Barclay, *Paul and the Gift* (Grand Rapids, MI: Eerdmans, 2015), 183.

Chapter 10: For the Life of the World

1. See James K. A. Smith's helpful explanation of Charles Taylor's assessment of the secular age and how we got here in *How (Not) to Be Secular: Reading Charles Taylor* (Grand Rapids, MI: Eerdmans, 2014).

2. I'm paraphrasing Smith here in *How (Not) to Be Secular,* 3.

3. This is, by the way, why Luke opened his "volume 2," the book of Acts, with a story of the disciples asking the risen Jesus if it was at *this* time that He would restore the kingdom to Israel—their hope had not changed, even if their time line had!

4. Flannery O'Connor, *Mystery and Manners: Occasional Prose* (New York: Macmillan, 1969), 44.

5. Smith, *How (Not) to Be Secular,* viii.

6. "Retractable Roof on Wimbledon Tennis Stadium," Design Build Network, www.designbuild-network.com/projects /wimbeldon-roof/.

7. Associated Press, "Wimbledon Roof Closes for First Time, ESPN, June 29, 2009, www.espn.com/sports/tennis /wimbledon09/news/story?id=4294536.

8. Bob Dylan, "Gotta Serve Somebody," *Slow Train Coming,* copyright © 1979, Columbia Records.

9. N. T. Wright, *The Challenge of Jesus: Rediscovering Who Jesus Was and Is* (Downers Grove, IL: InterVarsity, 1999), 189–91.

Chapter 11: The King's Feast

1. The twelve baskets were no accident either; they were meant to point to the twelve tribes of Israel, indicating that only when we embrace Jesus as our true king will there be more than enough for everyone.

2. St. Augustine, *Confessions,* in *Nicene and Post-Nicene Fathers: First Series,* ed. Philip Schaff, vol. 1, *The Confessions and Letters of St. Augustine* (New York: Cosimo Classics, 2007), 45.

3. George Marsden, *Jonathan Edwards: A Life* (New Haven, CT: Yale University Press, 2004), 463.

4. I am indebted to Ashley Null's marvelous reflections on the Comfortable Words in *Divine Allurement: Cranmer's Comfortable Words* (London: Latimer Trust, 2014).

5. Ashley Null, "5 Reasons Reformation Anglicanism Is Relevant," The Gospel Coalition, April 18, 2017, www.thegospelcoalition.org/article/five-reasons-reformation-anglicanism-relevant/.